THE
EVERYTHING KIDS' ASTRONOMY
BOOK

Blast into outer space with stellar facts,
intergalactic trivia, and out-of-this-world puzzles

Kathi Wagner and Sheryl Racine

Aadamsmedia
Avon, Massachusetts

DIRECTOR OF INNOVATION Paula Munier

EDITORIAL DIRECTOR Laura M. Daly

EXECUTIVE EDITOR, SERIES BOOKS Brielle K. Matson

ASSOCIATE COPY CHIEF Sheila Zwiebel

ACQUISITIONS EDITOR Kerry Smith

DEVELOPMENT EDITOR Katie McDonough

PRODUCTION EDITOR Casey Ebert

An Everything® Series Book.
Everything® and everything.com® are registered trademarks of F+W Media, Inc.

Published by Adams Media, a division of F+W Media, Inc.
57 Littlefield Street, Avon, MA 02322. U.S.A.
www.adamsmedia.com

ISBN 10: 1-59869-544-4
ISBN 13: 978-1-59869-544-1

Printed by RR Donnelley, Harrisonburg, VA, U.S.

10   9   8   7   6

July 2012

This publication is designed to provide accurate and authoritative information with regard to the subject matter covered. It is sold with the understanding that the publisher is not engaged in rendering legal, accounting, or other professional advice. If legal advice or other expert assistance is required, the services of a competent professional person should be sought.
—From a *Declaration of Principles* jointly adopted by a Committee of the American Bar Association and a Committee of Publishers and Associations

Many of the designations used by manufacturers and sellers to distinguish their products are claimed as trademarks. When those designations appear in this book and Adams Media was aware of a trademark claim, the designations have been printed with initial capital letters.

Cover illustrations by Dana Regan.
Interior illlustrations by Kurt Dolber.
Puzzles by Beth L. Blair.

This book is available at quantity discounts for bulk purchases.
For information, please call 1-800-289-0963.

See the entire Everything® series at *www.everything.com.*

Contents

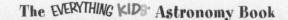
The EVERYTHING KIDS' Astronomy Book

DEDICATION
To Marcia, who believes.

Acknowledgments
Thanks to Mrs. Blomstedt for taking the time to share the skies,
and for quenching our endless thirst for knowledge.

Introduction

Blast off to a new world with *The Everything®
Kids' Astronomy Book!* Every chapter offers
a new adventure with places never before
touched by humans and others that have never been
seen, yet they are all out there just waiting for you.
Page by page you can discover what lies beyond the
world you know so well, and maybe even who might
be out there, if anyone. So grab a friend and prepare
to launch your way to nearby planets or faraway
galaxies.

Will you choose to go where no one else dares to go, like the mysterious black holes and potential time warps? Or how about taking
an eighty-year journey with a comet? Maybe you can solve all the
unanswered questions of time and space and why light travels the
way that it does. There are tons of activities to explore space and to
see how it feels to float free of gravity. Your journey into space starts
inside this book where you and your family and friends will find
games and activities that will challenge your mind and your skills as
astronomers and astronauts. Together you can cook up edible planets, create your own black holes, and possibly invent a new type
of candy bar. Or maybe you will want to invent your own alien or
become stars. Who knows, you may be the one to solve the mystery
of dark matter or find where the universe starts or stops.

In the pages of this book you will find information on how to build
your own sky-watching kit and how to change your room into a small
universe. You can also find out why people thought the sun circled
the earth and how they discovered the truth. Each chapter is jam-
packed with plenty of questions you can use to stump your friends
while you explore the skies and rocket away to endless galaxies. For
fun, you can experience the life of an astronaut first hand at your
own astronaut party. Together you can travel through time to a place

few people have gone, and learn what the future may hold for every-one who lives in our universe.

Before you are through, you can take a trip to the far side of the moon, discover what makes Neptune so stormy, and explore the world of the extraterrestrial to see why some people think aliens could exist. It will be easy to impress your friends and family as you learn how to locate stars and the many other things in the sky. Everyone will enjoy tasting a part of space when you make an edible planet. And who wouldn't like spending some time outside under the stars? So get out your blanket, find a pair of binoculars, and join in the fun of unraveling the mysteries of space!

Chapter 1

The Universe and Beyond

WORDS to KNOW

UNIVERSE: The universe is everything around us as far as the eye can see. It contains stars, galaxies, planets, space, and us. Some people think there are other universes that go on beyond the one where we live.

One of the first songs many children learn to sing is "Twinkle, Twinkle Little Star," but have you ever thought about the second line in the song: "How I wonder what you are?" Long before you knew what a star really was, you could see them shining in the sky at night. If you have ever tried to count all those stars, you probably guessed that there were a few hundred of them.

More Than Meets the Eye

One way to count all the stars in the universe would be to count so many each night, but don't expect to find them in the same place at the same time. If two weeks have gone by, start looking for them an hour earlier. Many years ago people noticed that the stars seemed to be in different places from time to time, so they believed that the stars were circling our earth. Now scientists know that as the earth moves in its orbit around the sun, different areas of the sky are revealed. The North Star is the only star in the Northern Hemisphere that does not move as clusters of stars circle around it.

Some people also began to wonder what might lie beyond the stars that they could see. As they studied the stars, they came to believe that the universe, the space around them, was composed of billions of star groups and each of these groups also contained billions of stars. Some scientists wondered, could there be even more stars? Could there be another universe beyond this one?

Long Ago

If you find it hard to believe that there are so many stars in the universe, just think about the number of people that live on our world. You know there are only

The EVERYTHING KIDS' Astronomy Book

a few people in your family and not many people live in your hometown. When you watch television, you see there are many people in other countries around the world, but does it seem possible that there are billions of people on our world since you never see all of them? Did you ever ride in a plane and as it flew higher and higher, discover how much more of the world you could see? It was always there, just like our universe, but you couldn't see it! If you asked a grownup why the plane stayed up in the air, he might have told you how he thought it worked or joked about his super powers holding it up there! You wouldn't believe that story or myth, but people living thousands of years ago believed that their gods were controlling everything here on Earth and in the skies. Some thought that a god rode the sun as it traveled across the sky; others named the stars and planets after their gods, and even referred to them as "heavenly bodies," as many people still do today. Each country developed its own myths. Some even made up stories about the shapes formed by the clusters of stars in the sky.

Imagine what your friends would say if you announced that a god lived on the moon and made the moon increase in size when it rose above the horizon and then made it shrink when it was high in the sky. Can you think of other myths you could tell each other? It does seem almost more like a story than something real, when you think about a universe born billions of years ago. Although the universe has been around for a long time, scientists think it

Going Backwards?

Scientists call the start of the universe "The Big Bang." What do they call the theory that when the universe ends it will collapse in on itself? To learn this name, color in the letters that are not Z, Y, or X. Then read the dark letters from left to right, and top to bottom.

Z T Y X H Y X
Y X E Z Z Y X Z
X Y Z X B Z Y X
X Z Z I X Y Z G
C Y X Y Z R X Z
Z X Y U X Y Z X
X N Z X X Y Y C
Z Y Z Y X H Y Z

may have formed very fast. Because the universe is constantly expanding, even the best experts can only guess how big the universe is or what shape it may be. Traveling millions and millions of light years to find the answers may take some time, but technology is getting us closer and closer each day. How big or what shape do you think the universe is?

The Big Picture

One way to see the world from a bird's-eye view is to visit a Web site that shows your town and house from space. At Web sites such as *www.terrafly.com*, you can view your house from the sky! The picture starts out above your town like a bird or the pilot of a plane might see it. As the picture zooms in closer, you can see each

house and the cars parked close by. To see this type of aerial map you can type in the words "aerial map" into your search box. Many of the sites offer you a chance to zoom in from space to your neighborhood or school. Another way to imagine how big the universe is would be to

How Big Is Big?

Astronomers figure that the universe has about 100 billion galaxies. If each galaxy has 100 billion stars, that adds up to a HUGE number—10 sextillion stars! Think about it this way: Ten thousand is a 10 followed by three zeroes, and ten million is a 10 followed by six zeroes. To find out how many zeroes are in 10 sextillion, break this number substitution (A=1, B=2, etc.) code.

20-5-14   6-15-12-12-15-23-5-4

2-25   20-23-5-14-20-25   15-14-5

26-5-18-15-5-19!

The EVERYTHING KIDS' Astronomy Book

take a map of your country and mark where you live on the map with a piece of chalk. Although your town may seem large to you, on most maps that cover large areas it will just be a dot. In a map of the universe, our planet would also be a small dot.

Countless Galaxies

Have you ever seen the Milky Way? This collection of stars can be seen all over the world; it looks like a ring of milk spilled across the sky. It is a small part of Earth's own Milky Way Galaxy, which contains billions of stars, and you can see it with your own two eyes. If you could see it from another galaxy, it would look like a pinwheel that rotates every couple of hundred million years. Other galaxies may look like a racetrack or a splatter of paint. Did you know that if someone gave you a penny and then doubled that amount each day, you would soon have more money than you could ever spend? The same is true for our galaxies; there are just too many to be counted.

Sailing, Sailing

The Milky Way Galaxy and other galaxies in the universe display many of the bright stars that sailors in ancient times used like the map your family uses when you go on vacation. These early stargazers were the first people to practice astronomy; they were studying the universe, although they could only see the brightest stars and a few of the planets. Today, sailors can travel over the seas using instruments that focus on the stars to guide them. If you are lucky enough to know someone that sails a boat, ask if they will show you how their instruments work.

Try This

Glow-in-the-Dark Galaxy

You can make your own spiral galaxy using a pinwheel and painting glow-in-the-dark or glitter paint on the top edges of each blade. Once it is dry, blow on the wheel to see how a spiral galaxy moves. If you used glow-in-the-dark paint, try it in a dark room. This is how our galaxy would look to someone out in space.

In the Neighborhood?

You may have heard of the Andromeda Galaxy, because it is fairly close to Earth, less than three million light years away. It can be seen without using binoculars on a clear night! Check your friends' knowledge of astronomy. Ask if they have ever heard of the two dwarf galaxies that can only be seen if you are in the Southern Hemisphere. They are known as the Large and Small Magellanic Clouds and seem to be held in place by the Milky Way's gravity! All of these galaxies, including the Milky Way, are part of what is known as the Local Group. Visit your local library and see how far away some of the distant galaxies would be! Weren't you surprised how many were scattered throughout the universe?

A Closer Look

Like the early astronomers, you may need to practice moving your binoculars closer or farther away from your eyes until you can see clearly. If you know someone who owns a pair of binoculars, ask them if they will let you look through them in the daytime. Can you see a street sign or a building that is far away from you? What is the smallest thing that you can recognize?

Round and Round They Go

Do you ever say the sun is "coming up"? It really does seem like the sun is traveling around our earth. The Greek astronomer, Ptolemy, thought the same thing almost 2,000 years ago; many centuries later, a stargazer named Copernicus claimed that our planet really circled or made an orbit around the sun! Each month you can see the shape of the moon change, but around 400 hundred years ago, a famous astronomer called Galileo was watching the changing shape of the planet Venus! This proved to him that it did revolve around the sun. You can go on the Internet and find pictures of Venus and learn when it would be the best time to view this phenomenon. Sometimes you can see it by using only a pair of binoculars. You probably already knew that the planets circle around the sun and that many of them have moons and rings that circle around them. But, did you know that our sun circles around the center of our galaxy? With so many things moving around here on Earth and out in the universe it is amazing so few things collide.

Observing Other Worlds

Do you like to take trips? Everyone likes to see what's beyond the curve in the road, over the top of the hill, or like Christopher Columbus, over the next horizon. Although you can't really visit them, now that you know about all these interesting planets, moons, and galaxies, wouldn't it be fun to take a closer look at them? Many cities have observatories that magnify what you can see with your eyes or binoculars and they welcome visitors. Maybe you have a smaller version of one of them in your hometown. If you can't do either of these things, look at a calendar, one that shows the full and little crescent moons. See when the moon will be dark; it's also called the new moon, because this is the best time to look at the stars and the galaxies. Make sure there are few clouds. Try to find a place where there aren't any streetlights. Then gather up some of these things you may want for your own sky-watching kit:

- A blanket, so that you can sit or lie down
- A set of binoculars, but try using only your eyes at first
- A compass to help you to find the North Star
- A pen and paper, so you can write down the stars you find
- Some snacks

See if you can borrow a star map from a grownup, so that you know where to begin to look for the stars. If

JUST for FUN

The Revolving Game

To do this activity you will need several children to be planets and moons. One person can be Earth, another will be the moon, another will be the sun, and others will be the other planets. Once you have everyone in place, start revolving. (The sun stands in the center, the planets spin and revolve around the sun, and any planets' moons revolve around them.) Remember that Earth will be spinning at the same time it is circling the sun. Now try trading places and do it again.

Which One?

Sir Isaac Newton first discovered the mystery of gravity when I almost fell on his head while he was sitting under a tree. *Which one am I?*

A. Orange

B. Acorn

C. Walnut

D. Apple

D. Apple

Try This

Going for a Spin

Ask an adult to tie a knot in a string and then thread it though a tennis ball. In an open area, hold on to the string and start spinning around; because of centrifugal force, the ball seems to pull more, the faster that you spin. When you get dizzy and stop, gravity will make the ball fall to the ground and probably you will, too.

you use a flashlight, the bright light may make it hard for you to see the stars after you turn it off, so be sure to cover the lens with red plastic wrap. Invite some friends and your family to go along, so they can enjoy the fun!

What Goes Up...

Have you heard the story about Isaac Newton and the apple that almost struck him as it fell to the ground? He wondered why it didn't remain in the air or even go up into the sky! Newton called the force that pulled the apple to the ground gravity.

After someone told you that the world was spinning, didn't it make you wonder why you weren't dizzy or why you didn't fly out into space when you jumped up in the air? Have you ever ridden on the flying swings at an amusement park? Before the ride starts, the swings hang down, but as soon the machine starts spinning, the swings move upward. The rider feels as though she is flying off into space; scientists call this centrifugal force. As the ride stops, gravity pulls the swings back down to the ground. How many other rides can you name that use centrifugal force and gravity to make you feel like you're in another world?

Balancing Act

Newton believed that gravity was also what held the moon close to the earth and the earth close to the sun. Like the swing on the ride, the moon is slowly moving out and away from our planet. The earth's rotation is gradually slowing, its gravitational pull is less, and the moon's spinning motion is moving it further out from the earth. Over time this has made our days longer. Scientists believe that, long ago, a day lasted several hours less than it does now. Gravity affects everything we do each day. Turning a corner too fast on your bicycle and landing on the ground afterwards is just one example of centrifugal force and gravity at work. Can you think of others?

A Real Balancing Act

Can you balance a ball on the palm of your hand? How about spinning it on the tip of your finger? It might be easier if you try twirling a coin on a tabletop. Balance is very important to all things in the world and in space. There needs to be just enough rain and sunshine for crops to grow, and there must also be a balance between the day and night. The universe seems to be based on a balance between push and pull. If gravity was too strong here on Earth, you could barely lift your feet to walk, which would be like walking through water. If we didn't have enough gravity, you might have to wear weights to keep you on the ground. Ask your family if you can wear a pair of their big

WORDS to KNOW

GRAVITY: Gravity is the force that pulls things toward the earth. There is also a gravitational force in many other areas throughout the universe that seems to hold things together.

boots or heavy shoes around for a few minutes to see how it would feel to have more weight pulling down on you. Having balance, especially balance in our gravity, is a wonderful thing.

One in a Billion

With billions of stars in the sky, it's not easy to find one star in particular! Can you find the five-pointed star that is hiding in this corner of the galaxy?

Taking the Long Way Around

Many galaxies are elliptical, shaped more like a racetrack than a circle. If you want to see if the stars on the inside edge of a galaxy would go around faster than the stars on the outside edge, challenge one of your friends at a nearby racetrack! Go around once and see if the one on the inside track wins. Then trade places to see if the one on the inside track still wins.

You'll Get a "Bang" Out of This

Have you ever placed a drop of water on one of those capsules with a foam sponge inside? Almost immediately, a foam animal appears. Now imagine that the capsule is smaller than a grain of sand and the foam is really made of super hot material that grows thousands, maybe millions or billions of times larger within seconds. Many scientists are uncertain if the creation of the universe was a quiet event like the growth of the sponge or if there was a "Big Bang" like fireworks, only louder, when it happened. Some believe that they know *when* the Big Bang happened because they have learned how to measure the age of the galaxies and the radiation created by the event that still lingers all around the edge of the universe. Just imagine if we were having a cake for the universe's birthday party, we would need around 15 billion candles!

Can you name the visible colors in a rainbow? Each color has a frequency wave, just like the numbers on your radio. Many astronomers use special instruments on their telescopes to determine which one of these colors or frequencies a star or a galaxy sends out. A redshift or low-frequency wave indicates that they are speeding away from the Milky Way Galaxy. If the redshift amount increases as you observe another galaxy (this means the other galaxy is moving even faster). If you were in another galaxy, it would seem as though our galaxy was speeding away from it. Does this make you wonder where the center of the universe really is? If you want to see an example of this, type in the words "Hubble & center of universe" in your search box on the Internet and see what you think!

Light Years Away

A farmer might think that a light year means that an ear of corn is smaller than last year, and a weatherman might use the words to tell you there wasn't

Sweet Scientists

Start at a letter marked with a dot. Collect every other letter as you spiral into the galaxy. When you get to the center, go back the way you came, collecting the unused letters until you reach the dot again. Write the letters, in order, in the spaces provided. When you are finished, you'll have three silly answers to the riddle!

What are astronomers' favorite candies?

JUST for FUN

It's in the Bag

Have you ever popped a balloon when it is full of air? Most astronomers think the big bang may have happened in a similar way. To see the force of the big bang at work, blow up a small brown paper bag and punch it until it pops. You might even have a contest to see who can pop their bag first.

a lot of rain in the last 365 days. Can you think of other meanings for the word "light"? An astronomer would be describing how many miles light would travel in a vacuum over the length of a year, which is over 5,000,000,000,000 miles! The spacecraft, Voyagers 1 and 2, after making a journey lasting for almost 30 years are just reaching the edge of the system that holds the sun and its planets. Light traveling at 186,000 miles per second would only take minutes to cover the same distance. If you would decide to become an astronomer right now, you might still be able to receive information from these ships for about fifteen more years! Even after we lose contact with these spacecraft, they could travel for many more years.

Do you like puzzles? If you do become an astronomer, maybe you will be able to find the answers to some of the questions about the universe. Even the most intelligent scientists admit that they don't know the exact size, shape, or age of the universe. They are still guessing about how it began or if the galaxies will continue to move away from the center of the universe. Do you think that eventually Newton's gravity will start pulling everything back into that small space where it all began?

Going Out with a Bang

If you have ever mixed baking soda with vinegar, you have seen how something fairly small can instantly become fairly large. It is thought that when the universe was born it started out small like a grain of sand but grew very quickly into the almost endless skies we gaze at today. The universe is constantly moving and spreading to places unknown. What could cause such a large explosion? Scientists have different theories of how the universe was formed, but most of them feel the big bang makes the most sense and explains all the things we are still seeing billions of years later.

Chapter 2

The Sun,
the Center of Our Solar System

JUST for FUN

Going Up?

If you want to know what it feels like to travel in space, take a ride in an elevator in the highest skyscraper you can find. Does your stomach feel strange when you come down? Another way to get this sensation is by riding a rollercoaster or swinging high in a swing. The reason you feel this way is for a short moment you are defying gravity.

A long, long time ago, astronomers always thought the earth was the center of the universe. But today, scientists know it is the sun that influences everything. As the planets developed around the sun, its gravity determined their size, orbits, climates, and even how long their days and years would be. Without the sun, life could not exist on Earth!

Too Hot to Handle

You might remember an instance when an adult told you never to look directly at the sun. But if you had to guess, what color would you say the sun is? Maybe you have watched the sun as it was setting in the sky. Sometimes it looks as though it is on fire, especially when it is shining through the clouds. The reason it looks that way is because the sun *is* on fire. Can you guess how hot the fire at the center of the sun is? It is more than 25 million degrees on the Fahrenheit scale! That's 250 thousand times hotter than the hottest summer day in Arizona. But what may surprise you even more is there are many stars in the universe that are thousands of times hotter than that. Have you ever wondered if it would be better if our sun's temperature were just a little warmer or cooler? Scientists believe that it is just right for us. The other planets in our solar system are good examples of what our world would be like if we were any closer or farther from the sun—or if the sun's temperature could be changed. Some stars are much hotter than the sun, which makes them burn up much faster. Fortunately, the sun is a cooler star that should be burning for many billions of years.

Out of the Dust

What would you expect to find in something called a nebula? If you guessed stardust, you were right! A nebula is misty or cloudy type of body that's filled with the gas and dust that was left in the universe after an old star or a supernova exploded. Something as simple as a bump from another explosion can cause gas and dust to start spinning around and picking up more material, resulting in this mass called a nebula.

Have you ever crushed the wrapper from a stick of gum? And did you notice that before you did that, the wrapper was several inches long, but after you have applied pressure, it was smaller than a pea? As a nebula is picking up more material, its gravity starts increasing and enormous pressure is placed on the center. It eventually becomes so hot that one particle of gas combines with another in a process called fusion! If you have ever watched a forest fire on TV, you know that a small spark can soon become an enormous fire. The fuel for the stars comes from hydrogen gas and it burns more quickly and much hotter than wood does. This star furnace can burn for millions or billions of years. But the hotter the fire is, the less time it burns. After it has used up all its hydrogen, the nebula may collapse inward, creating a very small star. Or it might explode outward, making another nebula filled with gas and dust. What do you think will happen next?

See for Yourself

If you visit an observatory, ask your tour guide to show you some of the many nebulae (that's the plural of "nebula," meaning many of them) that are scattered throughout the universe—such as the Horsehead, the Crab, and the Rosette. Some of them you can see because another star's light illuminates their dust, but astronomers have to guess where some of the other ones are because they are blocked by the light coming from other stars around them!

WORDS to KNOW

NEBULA: Nebulae can be both light and dark. If a star is shining on the nebula's dust or is inside it, it will appear light. Sometimes a nebula will block the light from a star that is behind it, making it appear dark or black.

FUN FACT

Gone But Not Forgotten

Astronomers have a name and a measurement for the amount of sunlight that never warms the earth because it is reflected back into the atmosphere. They call this unused sunlight albedo.

A Source of Energy

Did you ever wonder what it would be like if we didn't have the sun? Have you ever noticed how much cooler it is at night (when the part of the earth you are on is not facing the sun) or when it rains for several days? You probably enjoy snow days when you can build snowmen, but when the ground is covered with snow, the sun's light can't reach the ground, which means the sun's energy is unable to be used and instead of heating the earth, it travels back out toward the universe. We need the sun's energy to grow food, heat our planet, and give us light.

Have you ever heard of the scientist Albert Einstein or his famous formula, $E=mc^2$? He used the letter 'c' in his equation to represent the speed of light. So if you take the speed of light (186,000 miles per second) times itself (186,000) or squared, it equals around 35 billion. He believed multiplying the mass of an object, (in this case, the sun's gas,) by c squared (c^2) (the speed of light times itself) revealed the amount of energy that was developed. When you multiply even a little mass by such a large amount, you have a lot of energy! By calculating all of this information, Mr. Einstein figured out that the hydrogen in the sun would be able to keep the world warm for a very, very long time. You can see the sun's energy in full force in the summer time. It's easy to see how hot the inside of a car is if it sits out in the sun, especially if the seats are dark-colored. For years people have been trying to find different ways to use the sun's energy and warming power. Some people use solar panels mounted on their roofs to let the sun warm their house. Can you think of other ways to use the sun's energy? Food is made from energy collected from the sun. Even petroleum products and coal were made from plants that used the sun's energy to grow many, many years ago! Sun warms the waters in the ocean to grow plants to feed the plankton that feed the littlest fish to the biggest ones. If you want to see the sun's energy at work, how about planting a sunflower? Just follow these easy steps:

1. First you will need a large, sunny garden spot.
2. Once you have located your spot, loosen the soil a few inches deep.
3. You will need sunflower seeds meant for planting.
4. Plant the seeds a couple of inches deep.
5. Water your seeds at the time you plant them, and then as needed, allowing the ground to dry a little between watering.
6. When your sunflower is several feet tall, watch to see what the flower does as the sun crosses the sky.

WORDS to KNOW

LUNAR: The word lunar means of or about the moon. Many calendars are based on the time it takes for the moon to travel around the earth. This time is called a lunar month.

Sitting in the Sun

On sunny days, you can sometimes find a turtle resting on a log above the water, a cat curled up on a windowsill, or a snake stretched out on a rock. What all of these animals have in common is they are warming themselves in the sun. Humans, like other animals, also like to be in the sun. Every summer you can see people flocking to the beach, hoping to catch some rays. Not only does the sun's warmth feel good, but small amounts of sunlight can also help to keep you healthy. One of the things people get from the sun is called vitamin D. To help everyone stay healthy, many companies add vitamin D to their milk and orange juice just in case you miss your daily dose of sunshine!

Have you ever counted the colors in the rainbow? These colors are the parts of the light rays that you can see, but the unseen light rays, called ultraviolet or UV, are the ones that burn your skin and cause sunburns. So, if you are going to be out in the sun for a while and you don't want to wind

Around and Around We Go

Start at the very center of our solar system, and travel out to the farthest edge. Be sure to visit all eight planets, and the dwarf-planet, Pluto!

The EVERYTHING KIDS' Astronomy Book

up red as a beet, you will want to put on some sunblock (also known as UV sunblocking lotion). It is important to keep applying it, especially if you go in and out of the water. Another way to help prevent burning is to stay out of the sun during the hottest part of the day (which is usually early to mid-afternoon).

Sun-sational Things

You have probably seen lots of rainbows; especially if you have learned when and where to look for them. It is easy to spy them right after a rain, if it rains in the morning not too long after the sun comes up or in the evening right before the sun goes down. Do you know what causes the brilliant colors? It's the sun shining through the moisture in the air after the rain has stopped. Another fun thing to watch for is sundogs, which look like colored lines curved around the sun when it is not too far above the horizon. Sundogs get their color from the ice particles that are floating in the air.

There are so many unusual and spectacular things to see. One example would be if you climbed up a mountain and stood on top of it; you might have seen a silhouette of your head on the clouds below you. The only way this could happen was if the sun was shining on your back and if the clouds below were filled with rain. Then your head's shadow might have a halo surrounding it, just like the moon does at times. These strange sightings called "the glory" are very rare. You can increase your chances of seeing this if you are ever flying in a plane and sitting in a window seat away from the sun. If you watch closely you may see the silhouette of your plane on the clouds below, with colored rings completely encircling it!

The Air You Breathe

Unless someone asks you to hold your breath, you probably never think about how lucky you are to be

JUST for FUN

It Was So Hot!

Maybe you have heard the expression "It was so hot, you could fry an egg!" Depending on the surface and where you live, sometimes you could. To see how hot the sun can make some things, lay a dark sock and a light sock in the sun. After ten minutes, check to see which one feels warmer. Which color of clothing do you think would keep you cooler?

Try This

Making Your Own Rainbow

If you don't want to have to wait until the conditions are just right to see a rainbow in the sky, turn on your water sprinkler to send waves of water back and forth through the air. Make sure the sun is shining behind the water, and start watching for the rainbows to appear in the moving water.

surrounded with just the right amount of oxygen in the atmosphere around you. The Earth's atmosphere not only provides air for us to breathe, but it also helps to regulate the temperature of the planet. The sun provides the heat the planet needs to stay warm, but it also causes the winds that cool it down again. If someone asked you about the atmosphere, you would probably be thinking about all the layers that surround the earth, especially the ozone layer that helps protect us from those UV rays. Did you know that all of those layers combined extend to around 300 miles up into the air? The weight of all those layers on your body is called atmospheric pressure. Do you feel tired at the end of the day from all of that weight? If you've ever taken a trip through the mountains, you may have felt it was harder to breathe when you got to the top of the peaks because oxygen also gets thinner as you travel up through the atmosphere. If you had to guess, do you think the atmospheric pressure would be higher or lower as you neared the mountain's top?

Before people started traveling in space, they wondered if the earth was the only place in the universe that had an atmosphere. Scientists now know that many of the planets in our solar system along with other objects in the universe have atmospheres. Because these atmospheres aren't filled with air like ours, but rather other combinations of gases, they would be very dangerous to a person's health. After many years of studying space, they still aren't sure that anywhere else has the right blend of gases that would allow people or animals to survive!

JUST for FUN

What Did You Call That?

Can you name some of the different winds that move over the earth? A cyclone is just one kind of wind that is very strong. Can you stump your family or friends by asking how many different winds they can think of?

Sunrise, Sunset

You may wonder, does every object spinning around in the solar system have periods of daylight and dark? Most of the planets, their moons, and the other rotating objects actually do. Earth's solar day, with one sunrise and sunset, takes twenty-four hours to complete. Mercury, on the other hand, has a sunrise and then must wait until its next year for the sunset! Earth rotates from the West to the East, but several of the planets don't. So if you landed on one of them, it would be just the opposite and you would see the sun rising in the West and setting in the East! Can you guess how many times a year the sun has a sunrise or sunset? If you said never, you're right. The sun is always shining itself, even you can't see it from where you are, so it never has a night. It takes less than thirty Earth days for the sun to complete a rotation around its own equator, while its poles take more than thirty days. Are you wondering how this can be? It's because the sun is made of gas.

If someone asked you what was the most interesting feature on the surface of the sun, what would you say? Most people would probably say the sun's spots.

Ribbons of Light

Explosions on the surface of the sun, called "solar flares," shoot enormous amounts of energy into space. When masses of particles from a solar flare hit Earth's atmosphere near the North Pole, they cause flickering ribbons of light to dance across the sky. Astronomers call this amazing sight the aurora borealis. Break the number code to learn the more familiar name!

Extra Fun: Color the ribbons below with thin vertical lines of colors. You can use any color you want — the aurora has them all!

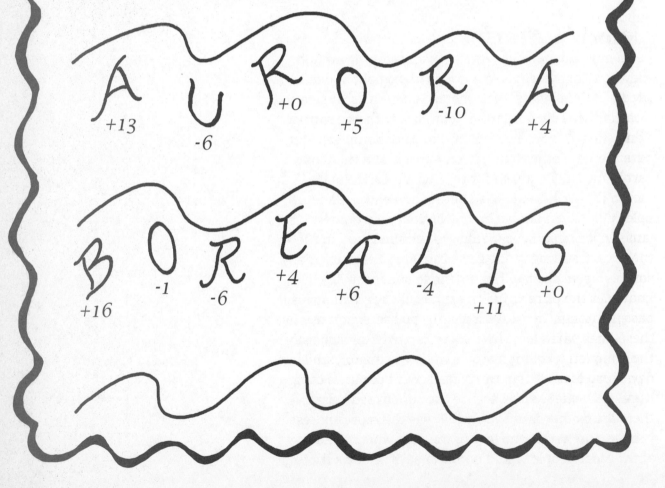

A +13   U -6   R +0   O +5   R -10   A +4

B +16   O -1   R -6   E +4   A +6   L -4   I +11   S +0

Astronomers keep a close eye on these sunspots, which seem to increase their numbers in approximately eleven-year cycles. These spots, which move across the surface of the sun, allow them to keep track of the number of rotations the sun makes. They think the spots are proof of an intense magnetic force that moves from the center of sun to the outside surface. Once it reaches the surface it radiates as energy to the rest of the solar system. This energy from the sun also creates a strong solar wind that cleaned the areas around the planets after they were formed and still carries magnetic particles to them.

Keeping Track of Time

Suppose that your family lost their way as they were driving across the country. What would they do? Most people carry a map to help them figure out where they are. They can also look at road signs and count the miles as they cross each intersection to find their location. On a larger map of the world, those intersections or lines are called latitudes and longitude! The parallel lines of latitude run east and west around the earth and start at the equator at 0 degrees. Slowly they increase to 90 degrees both north and south at the poles. All the parallel lines of longitude, called meridians, run north and south from pole to pole, across the equator, dividing the earth into sections that look sort of like an orange. The 0-degree point for longitude, known as the prime meridian, crosses the equator and passes through London, England. If you keep crossing these lines what do you think happens? Depending on the direction you are traveling, you will lose or gain a day. If you look at a globe, you can count the lines of latitude. Each one is equal to one hour of our solar day, so there are twenty-four sections. Pretend that it is noon in London. Then, if you travel westward, it will be noon at the place where you cross the next line; as you keep

crossing the lines of longitude, in twenty-four hours it would be noon in London again. The strange thing is, it would be a day earlier! That's why they put the International Date Line, where the date actually changes, out in the middle of the Pacific Ocean where it won't cause so many problems.

Are You Scared of the Dark?

Imagine if there were no television and no radio and you knew very few people. If that wouldn't be strange enough, then the sky starts to darken, the birds head for their nests, and suddenly the sun disappears! Would you know what was happening? It's no wonder that some of the earth's early inhabitants feared that this was a sign their gods were unhappy. To be sure they would have some kind of warning before this happened again, they built temples and machines to help them predict when the next eclipse or darkening of the sun might occur. Fortunately, solar eclipses don't last long— only around seven minutes. Eclipses of the sun occur when the earth, the moon, and the sun are directly in line with each other. Even though the diameter or distance across the moon is much smaller than the diameter of the sun, the distance between the earth and the moon allows the entire surface of the sun to be hidden from sight. Any type of solar eclipse can only be seen from a small area on Earth, so observers are usually glad even to see a partial eclipse where it looks as though the moon has taken a bite out of the sun! Because an eclipse moves so quickly, a person would have to run over a thousand miles an hour just to outrun the shadow it makes as it moves across the earth.

Yes, the Earth Is Round!

Maybe you have seen an eclipse of the moon. Since they occur at night and the moon doesn't turn black, it probably wasn't as scary for the early people as a solar

Free Vacation

Did you know that every person who lives on Earth gets a free vacation every year? That's right—no matter how rich or how poor, each person gets a free ticket to travel more than 370 million miles! Where are we all going? To find out, color in all the blocks with the letters F-R-E-E T-R-I-P.

```
F E E A F B W A F H T R X B F R E H T M F K M U T H F R
R A R B R E X B R J R K Y C V I K J R J R F J E R J R S
E B F C T D E C P K I F Z D Y P L K I H E S E K I K E E
E C P D R K A T I L P Y Q K Z T M L P J T D U L P L T S
T R I K I G B H R M T R S G Q F N M F K R C J G F M R T
A S Y G W H V J O N O B U H S H N N O L S H K G C N B X
T E F H F I H K R I T C F A F J T O K M F J R T A A C Y
R B R A R B P L I K R D R B R K R F L N R K R K T B D Z
I R E B E I H M P L I K E C I L I B R S E L E L R C K Q
P K E C T D E N F M P G E D T M P A X E E M E M I D G S
F L P D R K E S R E F H R E R N F S Y O E N F F X G H U
B M W K X G O H O H X A H G K G H J Z K X O M O Y H A V
F R E G T H F J T F Y B J F R E J F Q R Y F G O Z R B T
C E X H R A R K R J Z C K T O W K R S I Z R T H Q I C R
D E Y A I F E L I R Q D L R E E L E U P Q E K R S P D I
A T Z B P B T M I O S K M S O T M T V E S E L U I R K S
B R Q C E D T N P R U G N I P T N R E F U T M G V I G P
```

Chapter 2: The Sun, the Center of Our Solar System

eclipse. Since you know what causes a solar eclipse, what do you think causes a lunar one? A lunar eclipse happens when the sun, the earth and the moon all line up together. When this happens, the earth keeps the sunlight from reaching the moon. Some of the very first astronomers decided that the earth had to be a round object when they saw the curved edge of the earth move across the face of the moon. If you would you like to see one of these rare sights, type in "eclipses & NASA" in your search box on the Internet. You will also find lists and catalogs there that will predict the dates of eclipses to come for thousands of years!

Long Nights, Short Days

Did you ever wonder why the days are longer in the summer and the nights are longer during the winter? If you live in a place where you can watch the sun set, you might try looking to see where the sun is in the sky on June 21st compared to December 21st. June 21st is known as the longest day of the year in the Northern Hemisphere. Some of the first explorers soon learned that the further north you travel, the longer the days last. Have you heard of the land of the midnight sun? This land is located near the North Pole and named this because you can still see the sun at midnight! Unlike June 21st, December 21st is the shortest day of the year. These two days are known as the summer and winter solstices or the days when the sun seems to stand still! You might think all of this was caused by the earth rotating to the north and south, but it is actually the earth's rotation around the sun that causes these changes. Have you ever played with a toy top or a gyroscope? The center that it spins on is straight up and down. Unlike a top, the earth's center of balance is tipped over 23 degrees. This is a very good thing, because as Earth moves around the sun, part of the year the sun shines directly on the Northern Hemisphere and part of the time it shines on the Southern Hemisphere.

Try This

Red Hot

The next time you go camping spend a little time watching the campfire. If you watch the flames closely, you will see different colored flames that show the level of heat. Blue flames are the hottest, followed by yellow, and then red, which are cooler than blue, but still hot enough to burn. Stars like our sun are coded by colors depending on how hot they are.

The EVERYTHING KIDS' Astronomy Book

Chapter 3

Home Sweet Home, Planet Earth

Which One?

I can make your hair stand on end, even when you're not scared. I am a type of electricity. *Which one am I?*

A. Magnetism

B. Friction

C. Solar

D. Static

D. Static

Out of all the stars in the universe and the planets in our solar system, only Earth seems to have been able to produce life! While other planets' magnetic fields protect them from dangerous particles, only Earth's atmosphere gives protection from the objects flying through space and provides moisture and oxygen. Everything about the earth is special: it's length of day and years, the way it is tilted in the sky, and its weather that keeps it from getting too hot or too cold. Undoubtedly it is the perfect planet!

You Get a Line and I'll Get a Pole

When your parents take you out to look out at the stars, have you ever noticed what shapes they look for in the sky? Some of the favorite ones to find are little and big dippers. The star found in the end of the handle of the Little Dipper is called Polaris or the North Star. The Big Dipper circles around this star throughout the year. Polaris is used like a compass by all kinds of travelers, because it seems to point to the North Pole. Will this always be true? Although pictures of Earth make it look like a perfectly round ball, in fact it bulges out a little at the equator and is a slightly squashed at the poles. Because of this, the earth, like a skater wearing baggy clothes, doesn't spin perfectly, it wobbles. After thousands of years of wobbling the earth will move enough that the North Pole will be pointing at another star! Can you guess what one it might be?

Opposites Attract

Have you ever played with the strong magnets that you use to fasten your artwork to the refrigerator? If you try to bring the backs of them together, you can feel the magnets pushing away from each other. If you move them to one side you'll find that they cling to each other. What you are seeing and feeling are called magnetic lines of force. This same type of energy also flows from the North and South Poles of another huge magnet we call Earth. For years people have tried to understand what made the world magnetic. When you brush your hair in the winter, you can usually hear electricity moving through it. This electricity we call static is made up of charged particles called ions, which are always ready to travel from one place to another, if conditions are right. Sending electricity through iron or rubbing iron across a permanent magnet can create a new magnet. Scientists believe that the earth has a melted iron core that spins in the center of it. As the earth moves, the electricity from these charged particles also moves around, just like static electricity in your hair. This movement of electricity causes the iron core to become magnetic. Electricity and magnetism work together and can move in waves throughout the universe.

WORDS to KNOW

POLARIS: Polaris is the name given to Earth's pole star. You can find Polaris by looking for a bright star in the northern sky. It is part of a constellation we call the Little Dipper.

They're All Around You!

The weird thing about electricity or magnetism is you can't see it. A few of the other electromagnetic waves that you can't see are radio,

Go to Jail

2 PROVED   CENTER 9

S 13
Y
S
T
E
M

T 4
H
E

W
A 6
S

T 8
H
E

7 NOT

S
O
L
A 12
R

T 11
H
E

T
H
A 3
T

HE 1

OF 10   EARTH 5

About 400 years ago, the astronomer Galileo proved something very important about the stars and planets. Because of this discovery, other scientists and many important leaders of the day thought Galileo was "dangerous." He was arrested and sent to jail! Use the numbers to read the words around the border in order. You will learn what it is that Galileo proved!

television, X-ray, ultraviolet (UV), and microwaves. One form of the waves that you can see is sunlight. The sun is also creating magnetism. If you want to see pictures of its magnetic lines of force that escape from the surface of the sun, you can look at a book about the sun or type in "sun & magnetic lines" in the search box of your Internet! Maybe you have one of the many toys that use magnets that allow you to draw pictures or write your name, then you can make it disappear as quickly as you made it appear. In most of these toys the magnet is in the wand that you hold in your hand, and your drawings appear when chunks of metal are pulled up toward the drawing board by the magnet. You may have also used magnetic letters or pictures that cling to metal surfaces like your refrigerator. Each dark sunspot, an enormous magnet that can be as big as the Earth, has a North Pole where its lines emerge from the surface of the sun and a South Pole where they reenter it. Sometimes people can't use their cell phones or watch shows on satellite TV because a cycle of sunspots is sending too much magnetism toward Earth. Scientists who have studied the sun believe that the sun reverses its magnetic poles about every twenty years. They also believe the earth may do the same thing, but there could be many thousands or millions of years between them. You might think that all the objects in the solar system come equipped with a magnet, but there is no magnetism on the moon, Mercury has very little, and none can be found on Venus or Mars!

Our Living Planet

If small bits of stardust can become an enormous sun, can they also turn into a planet? Some people believe that when the sun was new and spinning, it took on the shape of an enormous whirling pizza with numerous lumps scattered throughout the dough. As the sun contracted, the outer parts of the pizza started to cool and separate and the lumps started to get bigger as they gathered more material from the leftovers. Have you ever watched a pizza maker spin a pizza as they were making it? When your parents place an order for pizza, see if you can come in early and watch this happen. If your parents make theirs at home, see if you can try your hand at learning how to spin one! Some scientists think that the sun burned away most of the gas that was around the lump that you know as Earth, leaving only rock and metal behind. Eventually dust that was created in the last moments of the other dying stars and mysterious balls of ice would bring to earth the materials it needed to sustain life. Their theory is that the oxygen created by volcanoes also combined with the hydrogen in the atmosphere causing continuous rain, which formed the oceans. After a long time, microscopic plants began to appear in the oceans and life on earth had begun. How do you think it all started?

Take a Look at That!

Have you ever watched a volcano erupt on a television program? All that red-hot liquid is coming from deep inside the earth! Do you know someone that has a lava lamp? They are fun to watch and they demonstrate how just a little heat can stir things up. The lamp's glass base contains wax and oil and the wax acts a lot like the lava in a volcano. There is a light bulb inside the bottom of the lamp that makes the wax melt and slowly float upward and then after it cools a little at the top of the lamp, it

WORDS to KNOW

SATELLITE: A satellite can be a manmade object or something created in space that orbits planets such as Earth. Manmade satellites are used to send information from place to place or keep track of the weather.

FUN FACT

Just Plain Shocking

Moving electricity through something creates magnetism, and moving magnets can also create electricity. They work together and are called electromagnetism. Electromagnetic waves are present throughout all parts of the universe.

sinks to the bottom and then is heated again. There is also a lot of heat in a volcano. Have you ever warmed your hands by rubbing them together? Imagine if your hands were enormous chunks of rock, like pieces of the earth's surface, moving very slowly over, under, and around one another. These chucks of rock called tectonic plates are like huge islands that cover the face of the earth. It creates a lot of heat and lava when one plate is forced beneath its neighbor. They can flow through small cracks in the surface of the earth anywhere there is an opening. If this melted rock finds a big enough opening, it can create a fiery fountain called a volcano. Do you think the layers of melted rock that ooze out beneath the plates on the ocean floor would match the earth's magnetic field? They do, but scientists have found some of the layers show that the South Pole was once located in the Arctic Ocean, which is now at the North Pole! They feel this discovery helps to prove that the earth has reversed its magnetic fields before, just like the sun does!

On the Move

Once in a while people will feel the ground move or hear dishes rattle in their cupboard. These movements are caused by the tectonic plates sliding against each other, causing earthquakes. Maybe you've tried tapping a glass or chunks of different kinds of metal to see what types of sounds they make. Scientists believe they can use the movement of waves from the earthquakes to show where the layers in the earth begin and end because each layer of the earth sends out a different type of wave. One way to think of the earth is like a peach. The crust or outer layer of the earth that you see every day is like

The EVERYTHING KIDS' Astronomy Book

the skin. Many scientists now think these earthquake waves show that under this outside layer is another layer of harder, heavier rock called the mantle, like the flesh of the peach; lava is formed in parts of this layer where the tectonic plates meet. Because there is so much pressure on the center of the earth, part of its iron core is a molten liquid. Way down in the middle of the earth is a solid metal core that is similar to the pit of a peach.

There's No Place Like It

Have you ever wanted to own a magical belt that you could strap around your waist to protect you as though you were a superhero? There are special belts out in space called Van Allen belts that are created by the earth's magnetic field. These belts work like a shield to protect the earth and everyone on it. The Van Allen belts are located above the atmosphere and trap dangerous electrified particles that are carried from the sun by the solar wind. Space travelers need special protection on their crafts as they pass through these belts. Some of the particles that escape from the belts near the North and South Poles can run into certain types of gases in the atmosphere. When this happens, sudden, fluttering, colored curtains of light seem to fall to the ground. These displays or colors in the sky are called northern lights or the aurora borealis when they appear in the Northern Hemisphere. They are known as the aurora australis when they happen in the Southern Hemisphere. The names for these lights come from the word aurora, meaning dawn. Different colors can appear when these collisions occur. If you hear of a lot of sunspot activity, you may want to watch the skies carefully, even if you don't live near the North or South Poles.

It's Just Right!

Do you remember the story called "The Three Bears?" and how Goldilocks kept looking until she

WORDS to KNOW

AURORA: One of nature's most spectacular light shows is called an aurora. These light shows take place close to the Northern and Southern poles of the earth as solar particles collide with the Earth's magnetic fields.

Going Around in Circles

Although the earth makes an oval, not a perfect circle, in its orbit around the sun, the earth's distance from the sun doesn't make that much difference in how warm or cold it is on earth.

found a place where everything was just right for her? You don't have to search very far to find the perfect place for you, because you and all your friends live on it. From space, our planet looks like a big blue-and-white colored marble and any traveler in space can see how fortunate Earth's inhabitants are to have all those white, fluffy clouds and all that water! One of the biggest mysteries in space is why Earth is the only planet in our solar system and perhaps the whole universe that has survived the "big bang" and is able to support life. What does make a planet just right? How many answers can you think of?

- Our sun is big enough to create enough gravity to hold all the planets in orbit.
- Our sun is old enough to warm the earth, without burning it up. All the other planets weren't as lucky; their distance from the sun makes them too hot or too cold!
- The earth turns every day, so that it doesn't cook one side while it freezes the other.

Some of the other planets' days last for many months on Earth.

- The earth is tipped a little, so it has seasons. No freezing or cooking!
- The earth is a magnet. This shields it from the deadly solar wind.
- The earth has a layer of carbon dioxide that keeps us warm.
- If the earth had not been able to make oxygen, there would be no oceans or air to breathe.

Astronomers have discovered there are other planets orbiting stars in distant galaxies, but they don't think you could live on any of them. Although many of the other planets in our solar system have mountains, sunrises, and sunsets, they don't have air or water. Do

you think they ever did? People use water every day for all kinds of things like taking a bath or watering their lawn. Water can also be used for fun. You can take a trip to the beach, canoe down a river, or ski down a mountain. Can you think of any other fun things to do with water?

What Time Is It Anyway?

If someone asked you when the sun usually rises or sets, you probably couldn't predict when it would happen unless you watched the news on TV. Many local meteorologists will tell what time they expect the sun to rise or set the next day. If you watched enough sunrises or sunsets, a pattern would start to appear and then you would soon know how much earlier or later to look for them. Do you think the sun rises or sets at the same time at places that are straight north or south of your home? Scientists believe thousands of years ago a group of stargazers built a place called Stonehenge in England to keep track of the sun and possibly other things in the sky. To do this they arranged huge stones in circles that seemed to use their placement to predict

Patience Please!

A quote about astronomers has been placed into a puzzle grid, cut apart, and scattered through the universe! Can you figure out where each piece goes and write the letters in the empty grid?

The EVERYTHING KIDS' Astronomy Book

when the sun would rise on the longest day of the year. Some people believe they also placed posts in holes to predict eclipses and to keep track of the passage of the days. At that time people didn't know the earth revolved around the sun, so how would they know how many days there should be? The mystery of Stonehenge is ongoing, with so many unanswered questions like were they counting the days till a certain star shape appeared again in the sky? Or when winter would come again? Over time people learned that the earth revolves every twenty-four hours giving us what is known as a solar day. They also figured out that it takes 365 days for the earth to orbit around the sun. Because there is 360 degrees in Earth's orbit around the sun and it takes 365 days to complete this orbit, the sun's star (sideral) day and the earth's day are almost the same length. Earth is one of the few planets where these two days are approximately equal!

The Passage of Time

One expression that best sums up fate is you have to be at the right place at the right time. That expression really holds true here on Earth. The earth hasn't always been the way it is now. Over four billion years ago, Earth was only a chunk of metal and rock, like Mercury is today. It took billions of years for the earth's volcanoes to fill the space around it with gases that would produce a protective atmosphere. The rains that eventually fell on the earth were made when two gases combined. This combination of gases produced H_2O, which is another name for water. The H stands for hydrogen and the O for oxygen. Another gas that formed on our planet was carbon dioxide. It took more than another two billion years, but animals eventually began to appear, too. Can you believe that this world, which had been steaming, eventually started freezing? Glaciers that covered much of the world would come and go for hundreds of thousands of years. Animals

Keeping Track of the Weather

Monitoring the weather can be fun. You can do this by making a rain gauge out of a clear plastic pop bottle marked in inches. You can also make a snow stick from a piece of wood or use a plastic ruler. How close are your measurements to those of the weather stations? Write down your measurements. Are they different each year?

WORDS to KNOW

METEOROLOGY: Meteorology is the study of the earth's atmosphere, usually involving activities within it such as the weather. Someone who studies meteorology is called a meteorologist.

Try This

Cloudy with a Chance of Rain

You can learn a lot about predicting the weather by looking at the clouds. Check out a book at your public library and memorize the cloud shapes and what they mean. Keep a record of how often you were right and teach your friends this new trick.

that were the first ancestors of your dog walked on Earth within a few hundred million years, but humans didn't appear until many years later. In many ways this may be the best of times in the history of Earth. What will the future bring? Only time will tell.

Predicting the Unpredictable

Meteorology is the field of science that studies the movements of weather all over our planet and in the atmosphere above it. Meteorologists use satellites out in space to track these changes and send the information to numerous computers. The computers help to predict what the weather might be across the country or near you. Did you ever notice how the sound of a train's horn changes as it approaches you and then goes on its way? Now imagine that the train is moving on a rainbow-colored track that starts out with a bluish color and then gradually becomes red. As the train passes you, it enters the red part of the track and moves away. Light and sound waves both look or sound different as something approaches or leaves them. Scientists call this the Doppler effect. Astronomers use it to track the movement of stars through red and blue shifts. When severe thunderstorms are around, your local meteorologist uses a Doppler radar to see if strong winds are moving closer or father away from you.

What do you think causes the weather? If you said "the water in the oceans," you would be on the right track. The main reason for this is the oceans store a lot of the heat that comes from the sun. Some parts of the ocean become warm enough to affect the weather on continents that are thousands of miles away. The sun also warms the continents, but when it gets dark, they get a lot colder. The difference in temperatures moves the air inland at night and then back out toward the ocean each day. One way to see this is by flying a kite. A kite should fly easily if you stand on the beach

8. _____

7. _____

6. _____

5. _____

4. _____

3. _____

2. _____

1. _____

SOLAR SYSTEM

NORTHERN MEMISPHERE

MILKY WAY GALAXY

ORION ARM

NORTH AMERICA

PLANET EARTH

UNIVERSE

YOUR STATE

YOU ARE HERE

It is always good to know your place in the universe! Can you put the place names that are scattered around the page in order from small to large?

— Write the name of the smallest place on line 1.

— Write the next bigger place on line 2.

— Keep going until you reach the biggest place on line 8!

HINT: Each swirling part of the Milky Way Galaxy is called an "arm."

around sunset. Then you can check to see if the wind direction really does change.

Our Ever-Changing Earth

There's a reason people say, "If you don't like the weather today, wait till tomorrow." Weather changes quickly, but the climate is usually unchanging. Or so it used to be. For fun ask your parents if the summers and the winters are warmer or colder than they used to be. A lot of the scientists who have studied the earth believe that the areas at the North and South Poles were flattened from the intense weight of the glaciers that used to cover much of the earth. Although no one wants another Ice Age, you might like a little more snow from time to time, so you can build an ice fort, skate, and ski. So why is the weather changing? You probably never thought that sunspots could cause so much trouble, but after a great deal of studying, it appears they can affect our weather! In the past, a decrease in sunspot activity may have lowered the temperature on Earth, caused droughts, and increased the number of storms. At that time, Earth may have appeared to look more like the moon. It's possible that the weather caused by movements in Earth's new atmosphere caused the craters on its surface to be flattened. If you were to travel to the bottom of the Grand Canyon in Arizona, you could see layers of rock that were created billions of years ago when the earth was new. It's like taking a trip back through time. If you wanted to see what a crater on the moon looks like, you could visit a place called the Barringer Crater, which is located in northern Arizona, or visit the Craters of the Moon National Monument in Idaho.

Chapter 4

Our Neighbor the Moon

People have always seemed to believe the moon was controlling their lives. In the past, they used it as a calendar and planted their crops according to the phases of the moon. Now people know it moves the tides in the oceans and affects how fast the earth turns. It may have once been a part of our world. Journeys to the moon by astronauts have given astronomers many answers to questions about our special satellite, but there are many more things they want to know.

The Man in the Moon

What do you see when you look at the moon? Is it a man's face or does it look more like some type of animal? Many people think they see what some say is the man in the moon. Others seem to see something else like a cow, which may have started the whole cow jumping over the moon story. Long ago, the Romans thought they saw the face of their goddess Luna. The images you see are created by the shadows that are cast from the mountains and the edges of craters. You might think that the best viewing time would be when the moon is full, but actually it is best to observe this earlier or later in the month when the moon isn't quite so bright. The early Romans thought the moon had a great influence on their lives, but scientists today know that it is the sun that has the greatest effect on life on Earth.

You certainly couldn't jump over the moon like the cow in the nursery rhyme, but did you know that you could jump six times higher off the ground if you lived on the moon? The moon is not only smaller than the earth, but it is made of much lighter materials, so

WORDS to KNOW

PHASE: When something changes or develops it usually goes through phases or stages. Each month the moon goes through a cycle of phases from a new moon to a full moon and back again. A crescent moon is one of the phases in the moon's cycle.

its gravity is a lot weaker! Some astronomers believe a chunk of the earth's surface may have been broken off by a collision with another planet when the solar system was first forming. The pieces eventually stuck together and then were pulled close to Earth by its gravity. This would explain why the earth and the moon appear to be the same age, but the moon's interior is so different. Before anyone landed on the moon, many people thought the moon was made of green cheese. Imagine their surprise when they discovered what they thought was cheese was possibly a piece of Earth.

Rings and Craters

If you like to look at the moon, you may have noticed from time to time something that looks like a halo or ring around the moon. Sometimes the ring is white, while other times it looks like a faint rainbow. A ring around the moon is caused by light shining through the moisture in the atmosphere, just like the rainbows you see here on Earth. Some people believe that this means that rain or snow is on the way. Another theory scientists have is that some of the rings on the moon appear to be circles of ice that line the craters lying close to the lunar ice caps. They believe the ice never melts there, because the sun's rays never reach that part of the moon. Unlike the earth, the moon isn't tilted. This makes the moon so cold that if you happened to be standing in a shadow, even when the sun was shining, you would still be freezing. The dark places on the moon are called mares or seas. Would you believe that originally astronomers thought the moon's craters were filled with water like the earth's oceans? For years people have been trying to solve the mystery of what caused these craters and why are there so many of them.

JUST for FUN

Astronaut for a Day

How about being an astronaut for day? All you need is some astronaut food like dry ice cream (that can be ordered off the Internet), cheese in a can, or juice in a box. To dress like an astronaut you will need a raincoat, helmet, boots, and gloves. Maybe your family can take you to a new place to explore!

Always Changing

Use the decoder to spell out each phase of the moon, below. Then, add up the numbers for each word and match the words with the description for each phase. Finally, color in each moon to show that phase!

39 = ○ *full of light*
60 = ◔ *between full and half*
22 = ◐ *half light, half dark*
67 = ◑ *a sliver of light*
32 = ● *all dark*

A = 1
B = 2
C = 3
E = 4
F = 5
G = 6
H = 7
I = 8
L = 9
M = 10
N = 11
O = 12
R = 13
S = 14
T = 15
U = 16
W = 17

5-16-9-9 *moon*

6-8-2-2-12-16-14 *moon*

7-1-9-5 *moon*

3-13-4-14-3-4-11-15 *moon*

11-4-17 *moon*

One reason they believe this happened is because the moon has very little atmosphere. Here on Earth, the atmosphere destroys most of the objects from space before they reach Earth's surface and leave their mark. The atmosphere also creates the weather, which has worn away the Earth's craters that were once much like today's craters on the moon. There are thousands of craters on the side of the moon that we can see. Over time astronomers have given names to most of them. The moon's craters are so large they would make the craters here on Earth look very small. Some of the craters on the moon are hundreds of miles across, while the ones here on Earth, like the one in Arizona, are less than a mile wide.

Now You See It, Now You Don't

Have you ever heard of a harvest moon? It earned its name from its golden color and how it seems to mysteriously appear in the fall, around harvest time. Unlike the sun, the moon sometimes seems unpredictable. You won't always find it in the same place in the sky at the same time each day. If you don't see the full moon rise in the East, do you really notice whether it's shining or not? There are times when the moon is shining up in the sky at the same time as the sun. When the moon is smaller, like a crescent or half of a moon, it doesn't put out as much light at night, which makes it less noticeable. If the moon is high in the sky during the daytime, few people see it. They may even mistake it for a small patch of cloud. As the full moon starts to grow smaller or wane, you will see half a moon, then a sliver of light, and then no moon at all. A waxing moon is when the moon gradually grows until it is full again. When you see the half moons, they are what people call the first and third quarters. Can you guess why? These phases of the moon are caused by the moon following a path around the earth, just like the earth does around the sun. At times the earth blocks the sun's light so it cannot reach the moon. When this happens you only see the part of the moon that the light shines on whether it is day or night. It takes twenty-nine and a half of our solar days for the moon to go around the earth. If you were able to be on another planet further out in the solar system, you could see the phases of the Earth just like we see the phases of the moon.

Making Waves

When people go to the ocean they almost always look for shells on the beach. The best time to look for them is in the morning. Did you ever wonder where they came from since they weren't there the night before? About every twelve hours the tides rise and fall, sweeping the bottom of the ocean as they go along. It might be hard to believe, but the ocean's tides have timetables on the Internet just like trains and airplanes. These tides are always changing because they are affected by the rotation of the earth and the moon. The moon affects many things here on Earth. Scientists like to keep an eye on the patterns and changes so they can predict what they call high tides. Why, you ask? In some places, like the Bay of Fundy off the eastern coast of Canada, the tides can change the level of the water around fifty feet; you wouldn't want to be standing on the beach with all that water rushing toward you! You may be wondering what has the strength to raise all that water on both sides of the earth? Although the sun's gravity has some effect, it is the gravity of the moon, even though it is hundreds of thousands of miles away, that exerts so much pull on the earth's surface. Over time, the moon's gravity has even slowed down the speed of the earth's rotation!

You might also be wondering if the earth is doing the same thing to the moon? Over the years, the earth's gravity has slowed the moon's rotation so much that it now turns at the same speed as it orbits the Earth causing us to see only one side of the moon.

By the Light of the Moon

For years people have wondered if a full moon really has any effect on people or animals. In an effort to find out, there have been many studies to see if animals are noisier or if people are more active due to the extra light the moon is reflecting on the earth during a full moon. Dogs and wolves like to howl at the moon, which may have started the stories about werewolves and other creatures that were affected by the fullness of the moon. One way to see if things are a little more active when the moon is full is to record the sounds outside. Then see if it is any louder on a night when the moon is full compared to a night when the moon is new and completely dark. Can you think of anything else that the fullness of the moon might affect?

Moon Signs

Not only did people notice over the years how the moon affects the ocean, they also started to wonder if it affected other things. Did things seem to grow better if you planted them during a certain time of the month? Before long, people started to keep track of these times, so they could better plan when to have their hair cut or plant their crops. If this sounds silly, it's not a lot different than listening to the weather before you travel and hoping the weather does what it is predicted to do. If you want to see if people can make educated guesses based on the phases of the moon, you can look in a book called an almanac and try planting something or getting your hair cut at the

WORDS to KNOW

REFLECTING: Normally, people are thinking of water or mirrors when they think about something reflecting an image or light. Even though the moon has no light source of its own, it shines in the sky because the sun's light is reflecting off of the moon's surface.

Hot and Cold

One day on the moon is equal to about two weeks here on Earth. The same is true for its night. Such long days and nights cause the moon to be both very hot and then very cold.

time they recommend. Then have someone in your family do the same thing on a different day to see whose plant or hair grows faster. Who knows, maybe years from now people will look back on these beliefs and think they were as silly as the moon being made of cheese?

Many Moons

You probably have never realized just how many times words linked with the moon or phrases based on your favorite satellite are mentioned in your daily life. Here are a few examples:

- Once in a blue moon means, "It's so rare it's not likely to happen!" Once in a while the moon can appear blue, especially after a really huge volcanic eruption. Bad forest fires can also make the moon look red.
- "Blue Moon," "Moonlight Bay," "It's Only a Paper Moon," and "By the Light of the Silvery Moon" are a few songs that contain the word moon. Ask your parents if they know the words.
- Several nursery rhymes such as the *Owl and the Pussy-cat*, *Hey Diddle*, *Diddle,* and *Winken*, *Blinken, and Nod* also talk about the moon. Do you know all the words to them?
- Monday is the day of the week that is named after the moon, and our calendar is divided into months, which are also linked to the moon.
- How many words do you know that start with the word moon, like moonflower, moonstone, moonstruck, or moonlight? Have you ever wondered why we don't have a moonrise or moonset?

On the Far Side of the Moon

Imagine how surprised the astronomers were when they learned the sun was turning. They figured this out when they started keeping track of the sunspots on its surface. They knew the sun was rotating, because the spots would disappear on one side and then reappear on the opposite edge. Yet, they were more surprised to realize the moon was rotating, because we only see one side of the moon. How could that be? After studying the moon for some time, they found out that it takes the same amount of time for the moon to orbit around the earth as it does for the moon to rotate. Both things take around 28 days, so we never actually see the moon turning around! The side of the moon we never see is called the far side. Every once in a while we do get a little peek at this far side, because the moon, like the earth, is round. During certain times of the month you can see around the edge of the moon as it makes its oval orbit, giving us a

Crazy Moon

A long time ago, people used the Latin word for moon (luna) to create a new word to describe someone they believed had been made crazy by the rays of the full moon. The crazy thing is that we still use this word today! The decoder will help you figure out this common word.

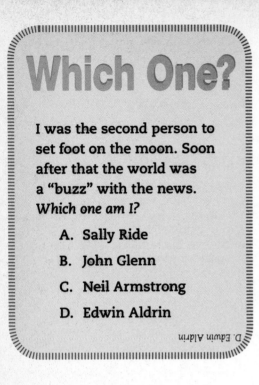

Which One?

I was the second person to set foot on the moon. Soon after that the world was a "buzz" with the news. Which one am I?

A. Sally Ride

B. John Glenn

C. Neil Armstrong

D. Edwin Aldrin

D. Edwin Aldrin

JUST for FUN

Lunar Party

Why not have a moon party? All you need is a few friends, some cheesy snacks, a bouncy obstacle course, and a place to gaze at the moon. Start your party early enough to have your games and challenges before it gets dark. When you plan your party make sure the moon is supposed to be out that night.

The Dark Side?

You don't want to make the mistake of calling the far side of the moon the dark side. Why? Because, there is no dark side, only a side that you can't see from Earth! You might expect the far side of the moon to look a lot like the side that we can see. In fact, pictures have been taken by space travelers revealing that they are quite different. Although there are craters all over both sides of the moon, there are very few maria or craters filled with volcanic rock on the far side. Visitors to the moon don't have to worry about the volcanoes, though, as they stopped erupting billions of years ago. There are many more highlands on the far side, which are similar to the crust on Earth. You might think you were looking at two different moons if you could see each side one at a time!

What Is a Satellite?

Can you remember when you first noticed there was a moon in the sky? Did you understand it was circling the earth? Astronomers that lived thousands of years ago believed that it was, but ancient maps reveal that they thought the sun was, too! The moon is a satellite of Earth, just as Earth and the other planets are satellites of the sun. How many moons do you think there are in the solar system? There are over a hundred and still counting. Who knows? Maybe in the future they will find more moons circling the planets that they have discovered orbiting around other stars. Many of the other moons in the solar system are much larger than the earth's moon. Some are even larger than a few of the planets, but none of them have a moon that is so close to the size of its planet like Earth's is. Although there may be more interest-ing moons than Earth's, none seem to have as much of an effect on their planets. It took a long time before the people on Earth decided they could build other satellites that could be as helpful to them as their natural satellite the moon. There have been thou-sands of artificial satellites placed in orbit by space-ships and rockets. Can you guess what some of them are used for each day? If you said forecasting the weather, you're right! They are also used for sending and receiving television and telephone signals, navi-gation, and many other things. Most of these satel-lites travel at a certain speed, to orbit the Earth in twenty-four hours, and at a certain altitude, around 22,000 miles, to remain in exactly in the same posi-tion above a certain spot on Earth.

FUN FACT

Rockets Away!

Hundreds of years ago, men developed rockets that work a lot like the fireworks that are used every Fourth of July. Extremely large ver-sions of these rockets are used to lift modern space-ships into orbit.

Blast Off

Almost fifty years ago, Russian scientists were able to create Sputnik, an artificial satellite that could orbit around the earth in less than two hours! It sent out a beeping noise that could be heard by radios all over the world. It wasn't long until they started wondering how could they possibly top this. Less than two years later, they put an unmanned space ship on the moon. Before long, Russian satellites were orbit-ing the moon and the world was able to see what the far side of the moon looked like! The race was on to see whether the USA or Russia would be the first to put a man on the moon. Numer-ous unmanned space missions prepared the way for the 1961 launching of a Russian astronaut named Yuri Gagarin into orbit around Earth. Alan Shepherd, an astronaut from the United States of America, made a suborbital space mission the same year. Within a year, John

WORDS to KNOW

ASTRONAUT: Explorers who travel out into space are known as astronauts. Some astronauts have become famous for taking the first steps in space or being the first woman or man to leave Earth's atmosphere.

Glenn had also orbited the earth. Spaceships named Mercury, Gemini, and Apollo carried the astronauts closer and closer to the target. Most people know Neil Armstrong was the first man to step onto the moon in 1969, but did you know that "Buzz" Aldrin was the second?

To the Moon

Just imagine what it must have been like landing the lunar module, jumping on the moon's surface, or riding along in the moon rover. How would you have decided which moon rocks to bring back to Earth? Being an astronaut is a hard job, but most astronauts will tell you it is the most awesome job in and out of this world. It's not too late to find out if being an astronaut is the job for you. Space flight is just beginning

How Many Moons?

Our moon is much smaller than the Earth. How much smaller? Complete the following equation to find out how many moons you would have to add together to equal one planet Earth.

_____ number of planets in our solar system

+_____ number of dwarf planets named "Pluto"

+_____ number of hours for one Earth rotation

+_____ number of full moons in a year

x _____ number of years in 24 months

- _____ number of letters in "moon phases"

= _____ number of moons to make one Earth

and it doesn't matter whether you are a boy or a girl, which is what Sally Ride proved when she was the first woman from the USA to orbit the earth! Learning all you can about the universe and the space programs is a great place to start. You might also want to watch a rocket launching and visit the NASA Web site for a list of what is required to become an astronaut.

Monkey Business

Although there were no people on the first missions into space, Russian satellites called Sputniks carried dogs, rodents, and even plants. Before small animals were sent into space, insects were being sent by rockets. Maybe you've had some insects you wouldn't mind sending flying into outer space! These scientists weren't bothered by these bugs, but instead they were checking to see how well the insects would survive in the weightlessness and radiation found in space. Only certain types of monkeys were chosen to travel in these space vehicles, because they could react a lot like a human. These monkeys were trained to perform some of the same tasks that the astronauts needed to do. Can you imagine what it must be like training these astronaut monkeys? People who work with monkeys will tell you that they have seen some pretty amazing things. Everyday monkeys are being trained to do the same things people do, like open a water bottle or get something out of the cupboard. Some of these monkeys end up helping people who can't do these things for themselves. Humans and animals have worked together for years, so it isn't surprising to think they would be a part of our space program. Many types of animals continue to be carried in modern space vehicles. Numerous animals are famous for their space flights. Do you think it's possible to take a fish into space?

One Foot in Front of the Other

No human had ever set foot on any other place in space until 1969 when two astronauts by the names of Neil Armstrong and Edwin (Buzz) Aldrin stepped on the surface of Earth's moon.

How would they keep it in the water? And would a blowfish still blow up, or would it do just the opposite? Having a chicken that lays eggs in space could prove to be a little interesting, too, especially if you were on the moon! Now that we know animals and plants can live in outer space, what plants and animals do you think they will choose to have at the future space stations? Would you take any weeds or broccoli if you were in charge? How about elephants or snakes? It would take a pretty tall rocket to carry a giraffe into space, and a really long one to get a killer whale out there. Do you think there will ever be a space zoo or circus? Space exploration offers so many cool possibilities!

The EVERYTHING KIDS' Astronomy Book

Chapter 5

Closest to the Sun

Long Night

One night on Venus lasts almost as long as a year here on Earth. Because it turns so slowly and it is closer to the sun, Venus's temperature can reach over eight times as warm as it is here on Earth.

TELESCOPE: Before the invention of the telescope, astronomers were unable to see many of the things that are far out in space. With the aid of very strong lenses in modern telescopes, we are able to see things we never dreamed possible.

Nine planets circle around the sun. Since the sun's temperature is so important to life on Earth, you might think that other planets lying close to the sun could also have life on them. Unfortunately, the heat from the sun burned up the atmospheres of Mercury and Venus that could have sustained life on those planets. Mars might have had some type of life in the past, but Jupiter's gravity would crush any life on this huge planet made of gas. The only hope for finding any type of life might be in an ocean on one of Jupiter's moons.

Mercury, a Planet Baked by the Sun

Do you like to eat baked potatoes? When the potatoes are fresh out of the oven, they are firm and round. But if you wait too long to eat them, you will find they are smaller and have lots of wrinkles. Scientists believe that Mercury, the planet closest to the sun, has always been a very hot planet. If Mercury did have an atmosphere it probably burned up long ago. Billions of years ago Mercury was bombarded by objects from space. All of this kept the molten planet from cooling off. Eventually, lava from the volcanoes filled the depressions in its surface that are known as plains. Over time Mercury's core started to cool down and the volcanoes became dormant. As the planet cooled, wrinkles similar to the ones on the potatoes appeared. Astronomers named these wrinkles scarps. One of the biggest puzzles the astronomers discovered when they were finally able to look at Mercury through a telescope was an enormous crater called the Caloris Basin. On the opposite side of the planet they also noticed a pile of jumbled rock that they believe might have been created when a large rock struck Mercury. If you could put a thermometer on Mercury, it would really get a workout, because Mercury is one of the hottest planets in the solar system. Not only is it extremely hot with temperatures reaching nearly 800 degrees Fahrenheit, but at times it can also be extremely cold. Because of this, its temperature can vary over 1,000 degrees. What makes it so hot? Sometimes Mercury's orbit takes it very close to the sun. Another reason is it faces the sun for close to a year before it starts to turn away. The strangest thing of all is how a planet that can be so unbearably hot appears to have polar ice caps.

To some, Mercury is considered to be an inferior planet. This isn't an insult, it just means it is closer to the sun than Earth. The same is also true for Venus. Because of their location, we can see their phases, just like we see the phases of the moon. With special equipment, astronomers can track them as they transit, or travel across the sun. You don't need a telescope to see both of these planets, but if you did, wouldn't it be nice if you could use numbers to find where they were in the sky. These numbers could be like addresses, similar to our latitude and longitude on Earth. Over time astronomers did develop a system like this, by pretending there is a celestial equator and North and South Poles that extend on from the ones on Earth. Using this system they are able to map our whole universe. The universe's latitude is called declination, which is marked off in degrees using the number zero on the equator. The universe's longitude is called right ascension. It divides the 360 degrees

Many Moons

An astronaut visiting Mars might see one of its moons, Phobos, appear to rise in the west, while Deimos, another moon, moves from east to west, just like Earth's moon.

Which One?

Some people might think I am the planet that likes jewelry, because, like Saturn, I have so many rings. *Which one am I?*

A. Mars

B. Earth

C. Jupiter

D. Venus

C. Jupiter

around the equator into twenty-four hourly segments of 15 degrees. When astronomers want to find a more precise location they divide these positions into smaller amounts using minutes and seconds. If you get the chance to visit an observatory, you might ask them if they can find a certain star or planet using these declination and right ascension coordinates or numbers.

Venus, Lost in the Clouds

Have you have heard anyone call Venus the evening star? It could also be called the morning star and so could Mercury. If you carefully search the sky, especially with binoculars, you should be able to see both of them if you look at just the right height above the horizon. Venus sets higher in the western sky than Mercury. Eventually, both of these planets will drop lower each day, until you can't see them at all. A little while later you will find them in the eastern sky in the early morning. Because the planets drop out of view you will never see all the phases of these planets.

Like a Sister

Are you a lot like the other people in your family? Astronomers used to think of Venus as the Earth's sister planet, mainly because they were about the same size and weight. If Earth seems to be an ideal planet, Venus would have to be the opposite. Why are they so different? Well, for starters, its bright light is caused by the reflection from its clouds. Unlike Earth's clouds, Venus's are made from sulfur that is floating in its atmosphere filled with heat-trapped carbon dioxide. On Earth, volcanoes helped to create oxygen. On Venus, volcanic gas creates a sulfuric acid rain. This rain is carried by winds that travel hundreds of miles per hour. Because of this harsh environment, space probes that were sent to investigate Venus didn't last long. The probes melted, were dissolved in acid, or were crushed by an atmospheric pressure that is almost one hundred times as heavy as Earth's! Could anything ever live there? To answer this question the probes were designed to send back pictures. The pictures showed raised areas that looked like continents, which left many scientists wondering if Venus ever had oceans. It is probably just as well that the astronauts haven't made it to Venus. Can you imagine living on a planet where the sun rises in the west? And if you think that would be weird, imagine staying in a place where there are less than two days in a year?

Venus Is Coming Up on the Inside!

Venus is not only similar to Earth in shape and size, but it is also the closest planet to Earth. Even though Venus spins backward as it rotates, it still orbits the sun in the same direction as the rest of the planets. All the planets in our solar system orbit the sun like racecars going around a track. Like racecars, planets don't orbit in a perfect circle, either. Hundreds of years ago, after astronomers finally admitted that the sun was the center of the solar system, they had a new mystery to solve. Somehow they wanted to figure out why the planets appeared to speed up and slow as they circled the sun. One day a scientist named Kepler developed a set of laws that seemed to provide the answers. The orbits were ellipses, so at times the planets were closer to the sun. As the planets near the sun they slow down and then speed up as they move away. A planet that is close to the sun takes much less time to complete an orbit. How long does it take for each planet to orbit the sun?

Go Mercury!

In Roman mythology, Mercury carried messages between the gods and goddesses, and was often pictured with wings on his hat and on his sandals.

Why did astronomers name the planet Mercury after this speedy messenger? See how quickly you can break the Vowel Shift Code to learn the answer!

=Marcory curclas tha

=son fistar thin iny

=ethar plinat un tha

=selir systam — enly

=aughty-aught diys!

- Mercury takes almost 88 days; Venus takes almost three times as long at 224 days.
- Everyone knows Earth's orbit takes 365 days, but Mars needs about twice that time to make an orbit at around 680 days.
- Jupiter takes close to 12 years and Saturn takes almost 30 years.
- It takes about 85 years before Uranus returns to its original place in space while Neptune doubles its orbit time at roughly 165 years.
- Tiny Pluto takes about 250 years to circle the sun!

Unlike racecars, the planets don't really bunch up as they round the track. If you want to see their orbits, type "Solar System Viewer" in your search box on the Internet to see it.

Mars, the Bright Red Planet

Have you ever left something metal outside, only to find that days later it was covered with rust? The same thing is true for Mars, because its surface is covered with sand dunes and rocks that have iron in them. When one of Mars's strong dust storms occurs, even the atmosphere fills with the rust. What do you think causes this rust? Space probes sent to explore Mars have found water in some of the clouds, but only small amounts of oxygen in the atmosphere. Some scientists believe that billions of years ago, Mars may have looked a lot like Earth does now with a similar atmosphere and oceans. They also think that not too long ago, there may have been water on the planet's surface. Or that there may still be some water underground or near Mars's poles. After studying this mysterious planet for some time, astronomers think they may be seeing icecaps on Mars. These icecaps appear to shrink and grow with the shifting temperatures caused by the changing seasons. They're not sure

FUN FACT

East or West, Which Is Best?

Is Mars really going backward? It actually just seems so to us because it moves east when it orbits the sun, but when Earth's orbit passes it on the inside, it looks like it is moving west for a while.

Mystery on Mars

Space probes send pictures back to Earth one bit of information at a time. Can you put all the pieces together to see the picture that has been sent from the surface of Mars? Find the box marked 1-A. Copy the pattern into box 1-A of the grid. Find box 2-A. Copy the pattern into box 2-A. Repeat until all the boxes are copied.

if what they are seeing is really water or just frozen carbon dioxide. If it is frozen carbon dioxide it would be like our dry ice here on Earth. Although Mars is too far away to visit in person, you can watch two rovers named Spirit and Opportunity travel over the Mars landscape using your computer. These rovers aren't able to travel very far, but maybe someday, larger ones manned by astronauts will visit Olympus Mons, a dead volcano located on Mars. Olympus Mons is believed to be at least three times higher than Earth's Mt. Everest. Why do you think its volcano is so much higher than any of our mountain peaks here on Earth? Maybe the weak gravity on Mars doesn't pull them downward like Earth's gravity does. While the astronauts are there they might also want to explore Valles Marineris, a valley that would make the Grand Canyon look very small. But most important of all, they could finally see if there was or is any water on Mars.

Say What?

It often pays off to listen very closely when someone is talking to you, especially if they are offering you something to eat. Otherwise what you thought was going to be a piece of pie might end up being a pizza pie! This kind of poor communication left generations of people thinking there were canals on Mars when what an Italian astronomer had been describing were actually channels in the landscape! Some people really wanted to believe that there was life on another planet, so they soon dreamed up that these canals were supplying water to settlements in the desert. Scientists hoped the inhabitants would look like a lot like humans, but it wasn't long before pictures of little green men and bug-eyed monsters were appearing in cartoons, books, movies, and eventually, on TV. Was there ever life on Mars, and if so, what did it look like? What size, shape, or attachments to a Martian's body could really be too impossible to imagine?

What do you think a Martian would look like? Have a group of your friends try their hand at drawing one and then choose which one you think could survive on Mars. Animals on Earth have adapted to all sorts of impossible living conditions like deep oceans where the weight of the water can equal the high atmospheric pressure on some planets, the scalding temperatures inside underwater volcanoes, and mountain tops with very little oxygen. Even Earth has some pretty unusual creatures. Can you and your friends name a few of them?

Giant Jupiter

Can you see Jupiter? Even though its orbit is far beyond those of the inner, rocky terrestrial planets, its size and yellow gas-filled clouds make it very easy to see. Only the moon and Venus outshine it! Although Jupiter seems like a large planet, it would take about 1,000 Jupiters to equal the equal size of the sun. Even so, Jupiter is bigger than all the rest of the planets in our solar system put together! Although Jupiter's most common gases are hydrogen and helium, just like the sun, it was probably not large or hot enough to ever come close to becoming a star. Have you watched the pictures of the white clouds swirling in our atmosphere on the weather channel? They show the highs and lows in our weather and sometimes the storms moving across Earth. If you go high enough, there are rivers of air moving around the planet. The bands of color on Jupiter show the same thing. They move in opposite directions and the colors are indicators of the temperatures and the kinds of chemicals in the atmosphere. What do you think that sulfur and ammonia would smell like? Some think it smells a lot like rotten eggs. Since the Great Red Spot circles in between the weather bands, what do you think it could be? It is an enormous storm, much larger than the hurricanes on Earth, that has been ongoing for hundreds of years. How

All in a Line

Every two years there is an event called an opposition, when Mars and Earth's orbits bring the planets near each other and the planets and the sun form a line across the sky. How about borrowing a telescope, so that you can see the icecaps and other geological features on Mars. In about ten years, they will be even closer so you can see Mars more easily!

JUST for FUN

Out of This World

Once you have seen some of the planets in the solar system, why not draw a few? All you need is a few pieces of black construction paper, some chalk, a little glitter, and hair spray. Draw your planet with the chalk, add a sprinkle of glitter, then spray and display it. Can you draw all of the planets?

would you know where the gas in the atmosphere ends and the planet begins? Astronomers don't believe that you would! The enormous pressure caused by its gravity turns the hydrogen close to Jupiter's rocklike core into a metallic liquid form, and the spinning planet uses this to create a huge magnet! It creates a particle shield much larger than Earth's Van Allen belt. Can you image the aurora created by this? You can see pictures on the Internet of this beautiful phenomenon that were taken by the Hubble telescope orbiting above Earth!

Years ago, some people thought the earth's moon should have been called its sister planet because it was so big. They thought Mars's moons were too small and appeared to be much older than their planet. So, what about Jupiter's moons? There are so many of them that astronomers are beginning to wonder if there shouldn't be a limit to how small a moon can be before it should be called something else. At this point a moon only needs to orbit a planet to be called a moon. Galileo used a homemade telescope to discover Jupiter's first four moons, which were named Io, Europa, Ganymede, and Callisto. If you can borrow a telescope, see if you can find them, too.

These moons travel in sync with their planet. All four moons are always facing Jupiter, just like Earth's moon. This is about the only thing these four moons have in common. Io has more volcanic activity than any other body in the solar system. This constant output also gives it the newest outer layer of any moon anywhere. Just when most astronomers had decided that there was little water anywhere but on Earth, they found out that three of Jupiter's moons contain ice. They think Europa's ice might be covering an ocean and wonder if there might be life in the water. Ganymede, which is the largest of any of the moons anywhere and larger than some planets, is also the only moon with magnetism. How

Deathly Dry

Venus and Earth are similar in size and in what they are made of, but there is a huge difference: About 70% of Earth is covered with water, while there is hardly any water on Venus! To learn just how little water, fill the empty spaces of the puzzle grid with the scrambled letters in the shaded boxes.

HINT: Each letter fits in the column directly underneath it, but not necessarily in the same order.

many moons does Jupiter really have? Can you find the answer?

What You See Is What You Get

If you have ever looked at a prism when the sun is shining through it, you can see a rainbow similar to ones that nature creates. As light goes through the prism, it creates a spectrum or bar of colors. Scientists discovered if they used artificial light to shine through a container filled with a chemical or element like hydrogen and through a prism, only parts of the colored bar would appear. Each chemical made a different pattern on the bar. These lines or patterns for each element are a lot like your fingerprint, unique to you, and they never change. A machine called a spectroscope changes the spacing of these colors to equal a certain wavelength, the same way each radio station has its

SPECTRUM: Scientists and astronomers use a spectroscope to see the breakdown or separation of light into a spectrum, the same colors created by light shining through a prism.

own frequency. Once astronomers mounted a spectroscope on their telescopes they could use the light from the stars and planets to tell them what elements each one contained. They soon discovered some of the other things a star's light could tell them. Things like the temperature and distance to the star, and even if it was moving away or coming closer. When something is moving, the colors on the bar shift to the left or right, changing the frequency a little.

What's in a Name?

When you look up into the sky on a dark night can you tell a star from a planet? Even the first astronomers noticed there was a difference. They called the planets that they could see moving about the sky the wanderers. These included Mercury, Venus, Earth, Mars, Jupiter, and Saturn. They thought the stars looked as though they were assigned places in a sky that moved and they noted how they seemed to twinkle. To them the planets must have looked like colored dots that appeared and disappeared almost magically. For many years, they thought Venus was two planets, one that appeared in the morning sky while the other appeared at twilight. It's no wonder they named them after their gods. Some of the names were Roman, some were Greek, and many of them had more than one name. As their moons were discovered, most astronomers started naming them after the children of these gods. When the moons of Uranus were found, they named them after characters in famous books. As they keep finding more and more moons astronomers have started giving them numbers instead of names. If you are wondering how they are finding so many new moons, it's because modern astronomers are continually taking pictures of the sky. When they compare these pictures they are able to see when something new is circling a planet. What would you name a moon if you discovered it?

my name is...

The EVERYTHING KIDS' Astronomy Book

Chapter 6

The Outer Limits

Astronomy is full of surprises. Until larger telescopes were produced, everyone believed only five planets orbited the sun. Then they discovered the rest of the huge gas planets. Saturn, Uranus, and Neptune all have rings like the ones that circle around Jupiter. Mysterious Uranus appears to be green and its axis points toward the sun, while a blue Neptune's weather is what most people talk about. Hidden beyond these giants is Pluto, a small icy ball that many people are now calling "the dwarf planet."

Saturn's Fascinating Rings

What planet is the most interesting to you? Saturn is a puzzling planet and has been since Galileo discovered it had "bumps" on its sides. When he first observed it, he thought he might be seeing three planets! As mysteriously as they appeared, these "bumps" disappeared, so he began to wonder if he had ever seen them at all! Later astronomers discovered that the bumps Galileo saw were actually numerous rings, with spaces in between them. Even today, people are still able to watch Saturn's bumps or rings appear to come and go. The reason we see this is Saturn has a tilt just like Earth does, so the rings seem to disappear when you are looking at its equator. Although Saturn is famous for its rings, it isn't the only planet with rings. All of the jovian or gas planets have them, which includes Jupiter, Uranus, and Neptune. One reason no one knew the other planets had rings is because Saturn's could be seen from Earth, but the others weren't seen until space probes found them. The probes also showed that

Light as a Feather

Saturn has been losing helium from its atmosphere and gaining it in the center of the planet. Astronomers have decided it is raining helium inside the planet, making it sort of like a large helium balloon.

Saturn had many thousands of rings and even more gaps in between them. They also found tiny moons that seem to keep the spaces between the rings open and other moons that appeared to attract the particles and hold them in the rings. You may be wondering what these particles are and how they got into the rings? Many of them appear to be made of ice and some of them appear bigger than boulders. If you remember that the earth and its moon developed bulges as they pulled on each other's surfaces, the same may be true for Saturn's less compact moons. If they are tugged close enough to the planet by its strong gravity, scientists believe the moons could be pulled apart. Others believe the particles are left over from the creation of the solar system. Most people who study astronomy admit they really don't know.

Can You Top This?

Did you ever play a game called "Can You Top This?" You pull an activity to do out of a hat, then others try to top it by adding more details, like hopping on one foot, while rubbing your head and patting your stomach, and so on. Even in space, it seems one thing is trying to out do another. For example, Saturn's moons come close to being even more interesting than its rings. As you study the outer planets it is almost as though Jupiter and Saturn were trying to form their own solar systems as they orbited around the sun. Only Jupiter's moon Ganymede is larger than Saturn's big moon, Titan, and both of them are bigger than Mars, Mercury, and Pluto. Most moons have little or no atmosphere, but Titan has a thicker atmosphere than Earth's. Have you ever seen a model of Earth, the other planets, and our moon? Imagine what Saturn's model would look like. A planet with thousands of bands of rings made from hundreds of thousands of pieces of rock or ice.

The Big Bucket

Saturn is huge but weighs so little that it could float in a bucket of water. Complete the equations to learn how big this bucket would need to be!

5	12	1	7	15
+3	-7	+3	-4	+1
-4	+2	+6	-2	-12
+3	-3	-2	+8	+4

The bucket would have to be more than this many miles wide!

AMAZING ASTRONOMY
The main rings of Saturn stretch more than a hundred thousand miles across space, but guess what? They are only 500 feet thick! That's like covering a soccer field with a single thickness of newspaper!

Astronomers knew most of the icy moons were there long before space probes sent back the news about the unknown tiny ones. Some of these moons are inside Saturn's rings. Two of them seem to be playing chase, switching orbits as they pass each other, while two or three other moons share the same orbit. Another little, strangely shaped moon speeds up and down as it rotates, while it spins like a child's top on its side! Saturn also has a medium-sized moon that seems to shine with an ice coating of water possibly due to geysers like Old Faithful, while most of the other moons are covered with craters. Can you imagine what a sight it would be to stand on Saturn and have five moons circling around you? Like here on Earth, Newton's gravity is controlling all of these objects as well, even telling the chasing moons when it is time to switch orbits!

WORDS to KNOW

AXIS: Like a top, each planet has a center line known as an axis that it revolves around. The Earth's axis would run from its North Pole straight through to its South Pole.

RETROGRADE: When a planet rotates from the east to the west or the opposite direction of the earth's rotation it is considered to be retrograde. Several planets in our solar system have a backward or retrograde rotation.

Uranus, the Tilted Planet

Would you believe Uranus's green color is not what really makes it such an unusual planet? As most of the planets follow their orbits around the sun, they spin or rotate on their axis, usually with their north poles pointing almost straight up. Uranus's North Pole, as it makes one part of an orbit, faces the sun, yet in another part of its orbit, the South Pole does. None of the astronomers seem to know when or how the planet's axis became tilted. If you could stand on either of the poles when they are facing the sun, the sun would appear to circle in the sky. Watching that would be enough to make anyone dizzy. As the year goes on, Uranus has equal days and nights then eventually the other pole has the sun circling around it. Because the North Pole lies below what would be Uranus's equator, its rotation is retrograde or backwards, which means the sun, as it gets further from the poles, rises in the West. Doesn't that make you wonder what clocks and calendars would look like on Uranus? It is probably a good thing that nobody lives there!

What Color Is the Sky?

Have you ever wondered why the sky is blue? When scientists studied the sky they realized the color blue was absorbed more by the atmosphere than any other, so that is the color you see when the sunlight reflects off of it. You may be wondering how can that be? Pretend that each color in the rainbow is a different sized ball with red as the smallest and violet as the biggest one. If the atmosphere lets all of the balls fall through it until only the blue and violet ones remain, the light will shine on those allowing you to only see blue light. So why isn't the sky purple? Because of the way our eyes work we see the blue better. Although most of Uranus's atmosphere is hydrogen and helium, it also has methane gas that cannot reflect red or yellow, so all that can be seen from Earth is a tiny greenish-blue dot! This is one thing that made it really hard to find Uranus. It was only by accident that Uranus was discovered; a stargazer who was looking for something else found it one night. At that time no one knew there was another planet. Maybe one day you will find a new planet.

Stormy Neptune

If you noticed a planet wobbling around the sun, wouldn't you start to wonder if there weren't many more? Astronomers started looking for another planet because Uranus's orbit wasn't a perfect ellipse. They decided only another unknown planet could pull its orbit so out of shape! Knowing it should be there and finding it were two different things. To find Neptune, they used the orbits of the planets they knew and calculated where it should be. This may sound simple, but it took over fifty years to find it. Even its unusual blue color didn't help, as Neptune can only be seen through a telescope. Have you ever seen pictures of a hurricane or a tornado? The winds in these storms seldom reach 300 miles per hour, yet they destroy almost everything in their paths. Now imagine living on Neptune where the wind is constantly moving over 1,000 miles an hour, everywhere. Great hurricane-like storms as big as the planet Earth are spotted frequently on Neptune's surface, but they quickly disappear. What causes all this stormy weather? Although Neptune does get a little heat from the sun and has seasons just like Earth, it is not enough to drive a weather system. Neptune's great storms come from the internal heat found deep inside the planet that clashes with the icy cold space surrounding it.

Going Back

How worried would you be if you thought the earth's moon was getting closer, instead of moving out into space? Neptune's moon, Triton, with its retrograde orbit, is steadily moving closer to the planet. If it keeps moving in the same direction it will probably be pulled apart millions of years from now. Over the years this has people wondering if other planets have captured or destroyed moons? After examining some of Neptune's moons, they certainly do look like they have been through some rough battles and many seem to appear as though they may come from other parts of the solar system. Just imagine if all the planets and moons could talk, what stories they would tell.

The Big Four Planets!

If someone asked you to describe a jovian or gas planet, where would you start? Most people would say, "They're long way from the sun, so they should be really cold." Other things that are true:

- Surprisingly, they all have some rock in their cores.

Long Journey

Neptune is located at the outer edge of our solar system, so it takes a long time to travel all the way around the sun. In fact, even though Neptune was discovered in 1846, it still has not made one complete orbit! Use the following rules to cross numbers out of the grid. The remaining number will tell you how many Earth-years equal one Neptune-year!

Cross out numbers...

...with two zeroes

...with three digits that add up to 8

...that are divisible by 2

200	620	222	1010
2030	305	422	611
910	500	161	125
341	2007	165	442
142	820	710	300

- It's hard to tell where their moving bands of atmosphere stop and each planet starts.
- Some of their atmospheres turn faster than the planet does.
- Although some of the planets' areas near their poles move faster than their equators, they all rotate faster than their terrestrial neighbors do.
- All four make a complete rotation on their axis in hours, even though it takes them years to complete an orbit around the sun. This may be due to a lack of friction.

You may have also said you thought the gas planets are big, which is very true. It would take you four times as long to circle around the smallest one, Neptune, as it would to go around Earth. One thing most people don't know is that the gas planets have magnetic qualities. The hardest thing to believe is astronomers think one of the planet's magnets might be made out of ammonia and water! Another difference is that gas planets have no craters. Of course, how could there be? About the only thing they have in common with the first four planets is that they have moons and they orbit the sun.

The Mystery of Pluto

Imagine that you dropped a tiny brown rock on a sandy beach. Do you think you would be able to find it again? Finding Pluto was just about that hard or maybe harder. Once astronomers realized there might be another planet disturbing Uranus's and Neptune's orbits, they started searching through thousands of stars each night with their telescopes to see if they could find it. Almost a hundred years passed before Pluto was discovered. The early stargazers called the planets "wanderers" and Pluto certainly lives up to that name. Sometimes Pluto's orbit is closer to the sun than Neptune's while other times it is the farthest planet

The EVERYTHING KIDS' Astronomy Book

out in the solar system, leaving people to wonder if the two planets will eventually destroy each other when their orbits cross. Just like so many of the moons that always face their planets, the orbits of Neptune and Pluto are exactly spaced or in sync, so the planets will probably never be in the same place at the same time! Pluto and its moon, Charon, are tidally locked like so many of the other moons and planets; they disappear and reappear as they eclipse each other. Even though Pluto orbits the sun and has a moon, it now is considered a dwarf planet because it is so small.

Planet X

There's a famous expression that "You should never jump to a conclusion," which is usually a good idea. But oddly enough, that's how an astronomer finally found Pluto! It literally jumped out at him. If you decided you wanted to find a planet, what would you think you would need to do? You would probably spend lots of time calculating where you think it should be, scan the skies, and take lots of pictures using your telescope. If you use a machine that can move quickly between the photographs of the same areas of space, and it makes that star you thought you were looking at appear to jump, maybe you have found a new planet! Do you believe Pluto was the planet that astronomers thought was affecting Uranus and Neptune's orbits or do you think there are more planets lurking even farther away from the sun? If it were about the same size as Pluto and as dark as most of the outer moons in the solar system are, would anyone see it? Do you think Pluto should still be called a planet? Many astronomers don't. If you are wondering why, it's because they think it escaped from the group of icy objects that circle the edge of the solar system. They also think there are more just waiting to be discovered. Maybe some of them are even bigger than Pluto!

WORDS to KNOW

DWARF PLANET: A dwarf planet is a planet that is smaller in size than the other planets it is being compared to. Pluto is considered a dwarf planet because it is so much smaller than the other planets in our solar system.

Making It Clear!

Does anyone in your family wear glasses? They probably got them because the right type of lenses makes their blurry vision sharp and clear. Galileo used similar lenses in his telescope because he wanted to do the same thing. The first lens acts like a prism by bending and concentrating the light it receives from space into a very small area; a second movable lens called the eyepiece lets you adjust the focus and enlarge the image you see. Your eyes and binoculars work in much the same way. Have you ever looked at yourself in a mirror in a funhouse? Sometimes things aren't always what they seem. A mirror can distort what you see but scientists have found ones that are molded to form a concave surface make the best telescopes. This type of reflecting telescope catches the light received from a star on its mirror, concentrates and focuses it much like the refracting telescope does, but the image is clearer. As the size of the mirrors in the observatories telescopes increase, the astronomers using them are able to see more distant, brighter stars. Mirrors in the Keck telescope in Hawaii are wider than a swimming pool!

Have you ever tried doing a regular activity, only doing the same thing while looking in a mirror? How about walking backwards or tying your shoe? You can probably see a telescope that uses mirrors at an observatory or a star party. If you think you would like information about observatories or star parties near you, type in skyandtelescope.com.

Star parties are a good place to find out whether you really are interested in astronomy and it might give you a chance to try out some equipment before you buy it.

The EVERYTHING KIDS' Astronomy Book

Poor Pluto!

When Pluto was discovered in 1930, it was called our ninth planet. But since then, astronomers have discovered other objects in the outer solar system that are similar to Pluto. In fact, some are even bigger than Pluto! In 2006, a special category was created for Pluto and its neighbors. Complete this puzzle to learn the name of this new category!

GALAXY   ASTEROID   SOLAR FLARE   SUN
MERCURY   JUPITER   MILKY WAY   MARS
EARTH   COMET   BIG DIPPER   VENUS

— Find the proper column for each word in the list. Watch out: There's an extra word!

— Write the words into the grid from top to bottom.

— Read the shaded row across.

Long Ago and Far Away!

If you decided to buy a telescope, you probably would pick out a refracting telescope, because you would be moving it around a lot. Do you think you could find new planets, stars, or even the edge of the universe if you just had a bigger telescope located in a better spot? Most telescopes are located on high mountains to avoid the atmosphere that causes the stars to twinkle. Astronomers wanting to avoid looking through the atmosphere at all used the Space Shuttle to put the Hubble telescope up above the atmosphere in 1990. They are now able to see objects that were formed over 13 billion light years ago, not long after the big bang created the universe. What is even more exciting is that you can hear the radiation created then if you use a radio telescope. Scientists discovered this radiation when they were perfecting communication

How many astronomers does it take to change a lightbulb?

Break the Last-to-First Code to find out!

oneN. stronomersA
anc ees tarss etterb
henw ti si arkd!

You gonna change that?

No way!

The EVERYTHING KIDS' Astronomy Book

satellites. Do you have a satellite dish for your TV? The dishes for radio telescopes look like much larger models of them. One that was built to scan the skies would cover a football field. Some are close to a quarter of a mile long! Some telescopes use a series of dishes linked together to get an even better signal!

X-ray Vision

You are probably familiar with having an X-ray if you've ever gotten hurt or if you have been sick enough to go to the hospital. Doctors use them all of the time to see inside someone's body. Dentists also use them to look inside your teeth. But did you know astronomers also use X-ray telescopes to see many things out in space that would not be visible using other types of telescopes? These telescopes actually see the X-rays that are given off by many of these stellar sources. X-ray telescopes have also been attached to exploration vehicles that were sent out into space. Eventually the images they receive will be sent back to Earth. By using a combination of several different types of telescopes, scientists are able to see the same thing in several different forms, allowing them to gain more information about the phenomena that they are studying. An X-ray telescope works a lot like your television. It can turn unseen energy into visible images. If you want to see more than you have ever seen before, try looking at your TV screen through a magnifying glass. You should be able to see the red, green, and blue dots or lines that form the true picture you see. By using telescopes and X-rays we are able to see things we wouldn't be able to see any other way. When the ability to use these X-ray devices became more popular, many people began to fear that eventually people would use these X-ray machines to see through everything, even into their

Imagine That!

Saturn appears to float in space. The lightest of the gas planets would float in an ocean like a beach ball if you could find an ocean large enough to hold this huge planet!

houses. They wondered what would happen if someone eventually invented a pair of X-ray glasses? And if they did, would they be able to use their X-ray vision to see anything and everything? It wasn't long before a comic book character appeared on the scene that could do that very thing. This superhero's special abilities came from outer space, and the only thing that could stop him also came from there.

Today, many types of machines can look into solid objects to see what is inside. Airports use a type of X-ray machine to see what people have in their luggage. This saves them time so they don't have to open each suitcase and pull all of the items out to inspect them. Would you like to have X-ray vision or a pair of X-ray glasses?

If you want to see what an actual X-ray image looks like today, you might ask your dentist or doctor if they will show you one the next time you visit their office. To keep you safe during an X-ray, medical technicians use special aprons to protect people from these invisible rays. Can you think of any other ways X-ray machines could help people find hidden objects or make our lives easier?

Chapter 7

Space Oddities

aybe you have seen comets and meteors speed across the sky or have heard that asteroids sometimes reach the earth. But did you know the universe also contains blinking lights called pulsars? These pulsars flash so regularly that you could almost set your watch by them. There are also black holes that can pull stars to their destruction, and a mysterious, dark unseen matter scattered throughout the universe. At the edge of the solar system are what astronomers think are millions of icy objects just waiting to become new comets.

In the Blink of an Eye

Do you like to read mysteries? Astronomy is one of the biggest mysteries of all because it is all about what happened and why. Do you remember what a supernova can do? If it explodes and nothing is left but stardust, someday it may become another star. But what if part of it collapses inward after the explosion? When it does happen, astronomers think a neutron star is instantly created. A neutron star is an object so massive that half of a teaspoonful could weigh as much as a million blue whales, the largest animal on Earth. If you think the magnets on your refrigerator are strong, imagine if you could squeeze that magnet to the size of a pinpoint. Scientists believe this compression is what really increases the magnetic field of the neutron star. Once the neutron star starts spinning, it sends out a radio signal. You probably think of your AM or FM radio as the only radio signals around, but your TV stations also use them as well as many other peo-

Picture This

See if your family has a camera that will take pictures of the night sky, or if they know someone who does. On a clear night try taking a few pictures of the sky right in a row. Later examine the pictures to see if anything changed from picture to picture. You could also start an album of amazing shots.

The EVERYTHING KIDS' Astronomy Book

ple like the police, firemen, truckers, and pilots. Have you ever felt the pulse in the inside of your wrist with your finger? Try to find it and count how many times a minute you can feel that beat. It should be regular like the pulse of a spinning neutron star, called a pulsar. Your heart probably beats at a different rate than your friend's. Each pulsar's signal also sends out a different rate and so its location can be identified if the radio beam is directed toward Earth. Try taking your pulse and the pulse of your friend each day for a week, and write down your numbers. Did they change?

Amazing Quasars

Now that you know that stars can be located by following a radio wave to the star, what would you do if you found a radio wave, but couldn't find the star? Like the astronomers, you would keep searching until you did! The light from the "star," although viewers on Earth can barely see it at all, is brighter than almost any other object in the sky and this indicates that it is a source of tremendous energy! How bright is this light? Brighter than a trillion suns! Astronomers have found out that they are actually quasars, quasi-stellar radio sources, and many of them are located at the farthest edge of the universe. By measuring the huge red shift in the spectrum of each quasar, they are able to determine how fast it is speeding away from Earth and how far away it is. Can you guess how far the quasar would have traveled in the time it has taken to read this book, especially since the universe is continually expanding? Scientists also wonder what else might be hiding near these mysterious quasars. Many astronomers believe they may be the centers of galaxies that cannot be seen by any type of telescopes. Are there still quasars in the universe today? No one can be sure due to how rapidly light travels; what we are seeing now may have happened billions of years ago! Do you think those quasars have been replaced by black holes? And do you ever wonder

FUN FACT

Flashing Lights

Lighthouses vary the pulses of their lights to identify their location. Some types of neutron stars are called "lighthouse models" because of the signal they send.

Now You See It, Now You Don't?

Black holes aren't the only things that can make stuff disappear. Try pouring water in a clear glass and adding a few of the following things to it one at a time like salt, sugar, baking soda, pepper, and flour. What happens? Now try testing a few other things. Which ones disappear?

Which One?

I have almost perfect timing. Some people say you could almost set a watch by me because of my flashy ways. *Which one am I?*

   A. Quasar

   B. Pulsar

   C. Asteroid

   D. Planet

B. Pulsar

if the universe keeps expanding, will the planets also get farther apart? Although that would seem logical, it doesn't appear to be the case. At this point in time the objects in our solar system seem to remain the same distance apart just as they always have been.

The Sky Is Falling

Have you ever watched the whirlpool that is made in your bathtub when the water drains out? A black hole is like a whirlpool in space, dragging any stars that pass close enough to their destruction. Do you know what powers a whirlpool? Gravity does! When a supernova collapses a heavy neutron star is formed. If that same star had been bigger, a smaller, heavier black hole with much more gravity would have been created. Astronomers have been able to prove neutron stars or pulsars exist because they send out radio waves, but a black hole's gravity is so strong it won't even let light escape from it. To be able to find a black hole, astronomers must look for its effect on other objects in the sky. Although X-ray radiation also cannot escape from a black hole, a star that circles it can have its gas pulled away. The radiation generated from the hot gas is transferred into the empty space beside it and this can be measured. Scientists have found the space is very small, but the gravitational pull is incredibly strong, so they believe they are seeing a black hole at work. Where would you look for the nearest black hole? Many of the stars in other galaxies appear to be orbiting around a huge, empty space. Maybe this is also what keeps Earth's Milky Way Galaxy spinning around.

Seeing in the Dark

Have you ever walked into a theater after the movie has started? Although you know it is filled with seats and other people, you really can't see anything but a

Name That Nebula

Over 200 years ago, astronomer Charles Messier was searching for comets. Instead, he found lots of fuzzy objects that looked like comets but were really star clusters, galaxies, and nebulae. Messier described these objects and their positions using numbers, but modern astronomers have given these deep sky objects more descriptive names! Figure out the picture puzzles to learn the names of nine of the nebulae on Messier's list.

big, bright, moving screen! Telescopes have revealed that the universe is filled with endless luminous galaxies, but most astronomers believe that the galaxies are surrounded by a dark halo or circle filled with dark matter. How did they discover the existence of this substance? Numerous calculations seem to prove there is too much gravity beyond the edge of each galaxy and throughout the universe for the amount of bodies of light that we are able to see! Scientists have come to question their original beliefs that all objects with gravitational pull must be visible. At this point in time astronomers can only guess what form this unseen matter might take. It might be dark galaxies, dwarf stars too faint to be seen, or black holes. Most scientists believe the dark matter formed right after the big bang and that it could be particles that are so tiny that they can't be seen or aren't able to send out enough radiation to be measured! Sounds hard to believe, doesn't it? Even after they have totaled up all the light and dark matter, there is still 70 percent of the gravity they can't explain in the universe. They believe that dark energy, the driving force for the expanding universe, accounts for the rest of it. One way to think of it is like magnetism or electricity. Just because you can't see it doesn't mean it isn't there. Until astronomers discover a way to measure it, they just have to believe it is there because they see its effect!

Misplaced in Space

Many years ago if you had asked an astronomer about space debris, he would have thought you were talking about stardust or chunks of planets and moons created when objects in space collided. Today, hazards in space are more likely to be manmade. With all you know about gravity, it is obvious that sooner or later, what goes up, must come down! Have you ever seen a really large meteor? Did you think that maybe it wasn't

The EVERYTHING KIDS' Astronomy Book

a meteor at all? Maybe it was junk that was left behind when it could no longer be used, such as:

- A piece of equipment or an item that came off a spaceship or astronaut;
- A rocket booster after it ran out of fuel;
- Or even part of a spacecraft or a satellite.

Old space stations have returned to and burned up in Earth's atmosphere after new, improved models have been lifted into space. Most of the tanks and other containers used for a shuttle liftoff never reach space. They fall into the ocean to be reused on another mission or burn up in the atmosphere. Parts of the rockets that were lifted above the atmosphere will probably drift in space for a long time. Are the remains of probes and spacecraft sent to other planets called inter-planetary trash? You can use satellites, the shuttle, the Hubble telescope, and the space station to practice finding objects in space with your telescope. Since they circle the Earth at regular intervals and at certain places in the sky, you can be sure they aren't meteors or junk!

In Search of a Planet!

Did you know that there over a million objects orbiting around the sun and they're not that far away? If you were an ancient stargazer and you found Mars and then Jupiter, you might have wondered why there wasn't another planet between them. When Ceres, an asteroid that is one-eighth the size of the Earth's moon, was discovered, they thought it was. Today's astronomers aren't sure if that space ever held a planet or if there just wasn't enough gravity to form one from the chunks of rock and metal circling in this asteroid belt. Some of these asteroids are as small as a compact car, while others are large enough for a spacecraft to land

Try This

The Sky Is the Limit

Some of the satellites or other man-made objects can be seen with the naked eye while at other times binoculars work better. Try looking through a telescope to see them with more detail. Keep a journal of your finds and start a friendly competition with your friends to see who finds the most objects!

on them, and one even has a volcano! How would you like to have been in the probe that did land on one called Eros several years ago?

Too Close for Comfort

Not all of the asteroids are between Mars and Jupiter—some actually circle in Jupiter's orbit and others cross Earth's orbit. These are called near-Earth asteroids. Several times during the last hundreds of millions of years on Earth, huge craters were created when these objects reached the planet. Many scientists believe that the shock waves created dust storms, volcanoes, and possibly some 65 million years ago, may have killed off the dinosaurs! There are satellites that continually scan the skies to keep track of where the asteroids are since a planet's gravity can pull them from their orbits. Each asteroid that they find is entered into a computer, so the scientists know where they should be and they continually monitor them to see if they are staying in the same orbit. You can help watch for asteroids outside the belt by using a star map and taking pictures of the sky. If a star seems to disappear, you might be seeing an asteroid crossing in front of it!

Showers from the Sky

How would you like to have a fireworks show delivered to your door? Check the newspaper and watch to see when the next meteor shower is coming! Astronomers know where to tell you to look because the meteors are usually pieces of comets that are located in one area of the sky at certain times of the year. The meteors are pulled in toward Earth as it follows its orbit around the sun. Have you ever wondered why we call them meteor showers rather than meteorite showers? Because up in space, they are called meteoroids, then they become meteors when they reach Earth's atmosphere, but they're not actually called meteorites until they hit the ground. Have you

The EVERYTHING KIDS' Astronomy Book

Oops!

If meteorites are chunks of space rock that hit planets, what do you call chunks of space rock that miss the planets? You must figure out the special way to hold the book to read the silly answer to this riddle!

Darn, I missed!

ever seen someone try to rub two sticks together to make a fire? What they are doing is creating friction, light, and heat. This is the same thing that happens as the meteors rush through the Earth's atmosphere.

What Was That?

Some meteors cause a sonic boom like a jet because they are moving so quickly. They can also burst into flame, and if they are large enough they can be seen in the daytime and are called fireballs or bolides. The best time for you to see a meteor shower is usually after midnight, so gather the kit you have for watching stars and be sure to ask an adult to join you. Meteors can be seen even when a shower isn't scheduled, so keep your eyes open. If you thought that you saw where a meteorite landed, would you know one if you found it? Some people like to try and find the pieces of a meteorite if they can

WORDS to KNOW

METEORITE: The objects that fall from space onto the earth are called meteorites. When they start to burn in the sky, they are sometimes called falling stars.

COMET: A comet is an object that appears to have a glowing tail as it travels through space. One famous comet is Halley's comet, known for its timely return trips

tell where a big one has fallen. They organize hunts and will sometimes let volunteers help them look. The hunters can learn where the meteorite came from by having an expert check it out. Most of them are made out of metal or stone, just like the rocks here on Earth, but they were created when the solar system was forming. They can come from other planets, the moon, and asteroids. Keep watching the skies and maybe you will get to help look for one. If you think you see one, be sure to tell your family and have them help you watch it. To learn more about meteorites, type in "museum & meteorites" to see pictures of them and a list of natural history museums that display them.

What's in a Name?

What's another name for a large meteor? Are they just small asteroids that have entered Earth's atmosphere? Some astronomers call Ceres a planetoid or a minor planet because of its size and the fact that it orbits the Earth. In astronomy's constantly changing vocabulary, today it might be called a small dwarf planet! What do you think Earth Grazers (EGAS) would be? If you said it's just another name for the near-Earth asteroids, you're right. Just to make it more confusing, some people also called the meteors that skim the top of the atmosphere and leave a long, glowing line the same thing. Have you heard the word binary, which means two of something? Astronomers use it when they are talking about stars, but there are also binary asteroids. When two people are born at the same time, we call them twins, even if they don't look exactly the same. The same is true for binary asteroids. Some of these asteroids have satellites that make an orbit around them just like our moon does around Earth! So when is a moon not a moon? Would you believe that many of the moons in the solar system are actually captured asteroids? Many of them are very small, have weird shapes, and travel backwards as they circle their planets. Many of the moons located in Saturn's rings are so small that they aren't called moons anymore; they've been downgraded or reduced in name to moonlets!

A Tale of a Tail

Have you heard of Halley's comet? It has made an appearance in Earth's solar system at around 76 year intervals for more than 2000 years! Do you know that you can actually see the orbit of the comet as it moves slowly across the sky, goes behind the sun, and appears again? This huge, dirt-filled snowball can't be seen when it starts the long journey at the edge of the solar system until the sun reflects off of it, just like the earth and the moon. Its long tail stretches across many millions of miles of the night sky as it is pushed away from the sun by the solar wind. Although the comet appears to be on fire, when its glowing tail passed over Earth in 1910 no one was injured. Some passing comets with longer orbits may not be seen again for hundreds of years and some never return. Would you like to have a space object named after you? Comets are usually named after the first person that discovered them. If you want to find your own comet, scan the skies and look for a fuzzy patch of light that seems to be in a slightly different area of the sky each night. Many stargazers have found comets with nothing more than a pair of binoculars! If you just want to look at one that someone else has discovered, ask your family to let you know when a comet is

Confusing Comets

This astronomer is searching for a special comet, but there seem to be a lot of choices! Which is the one he wants? Use the clues to find out!

The correct comet...

...must have 4 tails

...must have the tails on the left side

...must be round

...must be smooth

Touched by the Sun

Comets are called sun grazers because they come so near to the sun as they go behind it before they start back out into the solar system.

OORT CLOUD: There is thought to be a type of cloud that encircles our solar system, known as an Oort cloud. This cloud is believed to be the birthplace of some of the icy comets that can be found traveling through our solar system.

scheduled to appear again. They can help you keep track of them and the other interesting events by reading astronomy magazines or checking *http://skychart.skytonight. com/observing/skychart/skychart.asp* on the Internet. The first time you visit this site you may need an adult to help you type in your location and time zone. (If you would rather use another site, that would be fine too.)

Out of This World

Imagine that you could take a ride on Halley's comet. You know that it circles around the sun, but where would you be going on the return trip? You would have to travel billions of miles from the sun, past Neptune, to the source of most of the short-period comets. You might think your destination would be Saturn's rings that are shaped like a plate and filled with thousands of icy snowballs known as Kuiper's Belt Objects. Many astronomers wonder if icy Pluto and many of the moons orbiting the gas planets came from here. Have you ever wondered why the comets started their journey? A planet's gravity may have tugged on them if they got too close or the comet could have been struck by debris passing through space. Your trip wouldn't stop here if you were riding a long-period comet. They take hundreds, some of them millions, of years to orbit the sun so you could travel trillions of miles to the edge of the solar system! You'd be traveling to the Oort cloud, which encircles the solar system completely. Its comets can come from any part of the sky, not just from one direction like shorter-period comets do. You won't see the Oort cloud on the Solar System Viewer on the Internet, because no one has really seen it, even with a telescope—astronomers just know it's there! Be sure to check out the other orbiting objects in space. Even though the solar system is really big, some of these things look like they come pretty close to each other! Do you think as the universe expands or contracts that it will effect the orbits or courses of all these objects?

Chapter 8

Starry, Starry, Night

JUST for FUN

Indoor Night Sky

To make an indoor sky, take a large piece of black plastic and draw the night sky on it with a silver paint pen. Use a pencil tip to make a hole for each star in the plastic so your stars will shine from the light outside. Tape the sky over the open end of a large appliance box. You will need a door in the box to get inside.

WORDS to KNOW

MAGNITUDE: The amount of light a star emits or gives off is called its magnitude. Astronomers measure the magnitude of the stars out in the universe by using a number system.

The first astronomers probably spent more time writing down what they saw than they did looking at the stars. Because they passed this information on to others, it was easier for the new stargazers to look for their own discoveries. Today's astronomers continue to learn more about the creation and destruction of stars. Visiting a planetarium is like taking a guided tour of the universe that may make you want to learn more about the stars, the constellations, and all the interesting things that are happening in astronomy today.

Diamonds in the Sky

When it starts to get dark each night, which are the first stars you see? The brightest ones, of course! Over 2,000 years ago, Hipparchus developed a numbering system, one through six, based on the apparent magnitude or brightness of the stars he saw from Earth. A first or number one magnitude star was 100 times brighter than the faint stars in the sixth class. Over time astronomers have found some objects can be brighter than a one, so they started using a minus sign to indicate how much light there seemed to be. Do you think there are numbers higher than six? With modern telescopes, stars can be listed up to a thirty! Hipparchus might have been surprised to see astronomers still use the information from his catalog today. Newer books have changed the amounts of a few of his numbers and many, many more stars have been added to his list. Suppose you and your friends are walking after dark and you see a light shining in the distance.

It could be a streetlight or a flashlight. How bright it is doesn't tell you much about the light, if you don't know how far away it is. Modern astronomers have learned how to measure the distance to a star and its apparent magnitude, or how bright it appears to us. They use both of these figures to determine the absolute magnitude or luminosity (true brightness) of a star. Scientists pretend that the sun and the other stars are all the same distance from the earth to figure their absolute magnitude. The sun has an apparent magnitude of −26.7 and absolute magnitude of 4.8. See what a difference a little distance makes!

Connecting the Dots

Have you ever seen what looks like animals or people hiding among the stars in the constellations? Ancient stargazers like the Chinese, Egyptians, Greeks, and people living in the Middle East saw some of these same creatures. Some believed they were gods and made up wonderful stories about them that are still retold today. Each of these groups of people had different names for the same clusters of stars or constellations. Sometimes some parts of one constellation were grouped with part of another, and many were never seen because none of the stargazers lived in the Southern Hemisphere. You might not be able see all of them, either. Eventually it was agreed that there were eighty-eight constellations in all, but many of the shapes had been changed. Do you really think Cygnus looks like a swan or Canis Minor and Major look like a pair of dogs? Although the stars that form the figures appear to be close in certain constellations, they may actually be billions of miles apart. And because they are moving, they might be in other constellations eventually. Like the imaginary

CONSTELLATION: A constellation is a group of stars that together form an image in the sky. One constellation that is well known is Orion.

celestial equator above Earth that helps astronomers locate objects in space, there is also an imaginary circle called an ecliptic. This circle is where the eclipses of the sun and the moon occur. Some of the constellations seem to move along this circle. This circle swings from 23.5 degrees north of the equator to 23.5 degrees south of the equator as the earth orbits around the sun. Would you call the Big Dipper a constellation? To most astronomers it is an asterism, or just part of the constellation known as the Great Bear or Ursa Major!

How the Constellations Got Their Names

Have you read a lot of fairy tales or watched them on TV? Most of these stories were written for children to enjoy, but they were also written to teach children good behavior and keep them safe. Their lessons were things like: don't talk to strangers, be honest and kind or you might be punished. Ancient storytellers told stories about what they thought they saw in the sky, from mighty hunters like Orion to magical animals like unicorns and winged horses, or even things like a harp and a cross.

What's Your Sign?

When people talk about constellations, do you think about the twelve symbols listed in the zodiac? Many people do because it's fun to talk about astrology. The history of astrology goes back for thousands of years, and there is more than one type of astrology. In some cases the month when you were born is what counts while others rely more on the year you were born. Depending on what year you were born you may be under the sign of the rat or the monkey, or one of the other ten animals. Some people still believe that the date of your birth has an effect on your life. As the earth orbits the sun, several constellations

E ☆ H ☆ K ☆ N ☆

S ★ T ☆ U ☆ Y ✳

Picture in the Sky

Use a white gel pen or white crayon to connect the numbers in order. The decoder will help you to spell out the name a Native American tribe used for this group of stars, long before it became known as the Big Dipper.

are visible in the night sky for about a month right along the ecliptic circle. The sign in the middle is considered the dominant or main sign. In the monthly astrology, if you were born in the first part of the month of March, Pisces would be your sign. The sun, the moon, and the planets all appear to move through these special constellations during the course of the year. Maybe you have heard of some of the signs like the crab or the twins. If you think you might want to use astrology to predict your future, remember all of the changes that have been made in the calendars over the years. March 5 was probably January 21 thousands of years ago.

WORDS to KNOW

ASTROLOGY: Astrology is a belief that stars and other objects in space can be used to predict future happenings or events. People who are born under certain signs are expected to display certain characteristics and qualities.

What's a Planetarium?

Have you ever been to a planetarium? As the lights dim in a large dome-shaped building, the presenter starts the projectors that create the images of the many

wonders in space. In some planetariums as the displays change, you can hear the sound of gears moving. Astronomers living around 2,000 years ago used similar gears in some of their simple machines. These machines were used to predict eclipses as they moved the models of the sun and the moon around. Some scientists believe they also showed the paths of the planets. As the show in the planetarium goes along, you soon see the star-filled sky displayed over your head; it changes to show the seasons of the year and the hemispheres on Earth. Going to a planetarium is sort of like climbing into a time machine as it shows you what the sky used to look like and how it might look in the future. You can even experience what it would be like to travel in a spaceship throughout the universe. Wouldn't it be great to have someone to point out the locations of these different stars when you are in your own yard? Learning where to look for constellations and planets is as simple as taking a trip to the planetarium, buying a planetarium program for your computer, or going on the Internet to look for star maps at Skyandtelescope.com.

Double Trouble

Did you ever wish that you had a twin? You probably wouldn't care if they didn't look exactly like you, as long as they were always there when you needed a friend. Astronomers believe many of the stars have twins. Sirius A, the brightest star in the sky, has a white dwarf companion about the size of Earth, called Sirius B. You might be wondering how astronomers decide if one really bright star is actually two? They look to see if part of the star seems to be blue or coming toward them while the other half is red or moving away. Alpha and Beta Centauri are close enough together to appear as one really bright star, but they

PLANETARIUM: A planetarium is a special building designed to display all the wonders of the solar system and outer space to an audience.

Twin Stars

Can you find the seven differences between this pair of twin stars?

are actually triplets if you include Earth's nearest neighbor, the faint Proxima Centauri. Other binary or twin stars are discovered because once in awhile they eclipse each other just like the moon does the earth.

Seeing Double?

Have you ever had a tug of war with your friends? Algol is often called the "demon star" because it is hidden at times by its aging companion star. It almost seems to be playing hide and seek with you. This red giant seems to be losing gas to its brighter twin because of their close orbits! A tug of war between twin stars is not that unusual, and sometimes the winner is not who you would expect it to be. A companion star is often found only by the effect it has on another star. One way to spot them is if they wobble from the pull of the unseen star's

Try This

Star Parties

Who doesn't want to be a star? For this party all you need are a few costumes, some sunglasses, a star cake, and a camera. Roll out the red carpet and have a few friends come over for some star trivia, treats, and pictures. Everyone should make a star with their name on it for their own door at home.

Chapter 8: Starry, Starry, Night

I can make things disappear and reappear simply by doing what I always do. *Which one am I?*

A. Eclipse

B. Supernova

C. Rocket

D. Comet

A. Eclipse

Try This

It's All Greek to Me!

How about trying something new like learning the Greek alphabet, which is used for many things besides naming stars? You can find it in an encyclopedia or on the Internet by typing in the words "Greek alphabet." Are there any other alphabets you would like to learn? How about the sign language alphabet?

gravity. Could the other star be a black hole? When you go to the planetarium, you might ask if they have to use two projectors to show these binary or "twin" stars. Maybe they will show videos of the real ones!

Naming Your Own Star

The first time you meet someone new, you learn the person's name. Stargazers like Ptolemy started naming the stars in the sky thousands of years ago to help identify and keep track of them. You might be surprised to know that many of the names the stars are called today came from Middle Eastern astronomers living thousands of years ago. Unfortunately the same star was known by a different name in other places in the world. Modern astronomers started adding Greek letters to the unnamed stars in the newly discovered constellations like some of those in the Southern Hemisphere. They would name the brightest star Alpha, the next would be Beta, and so on until they ran out of stars or letters! This is not a foolproof way to know which are the brightest stars though, because the astronomers didn't want to change their names even after they found out the stars weren't quite as bright as earlier astronomers thought they were.

Some countries have tried naming newly discovered stars after their celebrities, but as you probably have noticed, there aren't any famous names listed on the star maps. Some astronomers have been honored for their discoveries by having their names used, but the newer stars just have initials that indicate the type of star they are, or numbers, or both. Now, when a star is found it is simply listed by its coordinates on the celestial sphere. If you want to find a new star, looking at catalogs that list the stars may help you. If you look closely, you may see the same star listed with its different names and numbers. Some day you might find a star that no one else has ever found before.

The EVERYTHING KIDS' Astronomy Book

Across the Sky

The word list is here to give you a hand, but be careful—there are two extra words!

NOVA
GALAXIES
RED GIANT
TWIN STARS
ECLIPSE

ASTEROID
COMET
SOLAR FLARE
MILKY WAY
STARS

PLANETS
METEORS
CONSTELLATION
TELESCOPE
FULL MOON

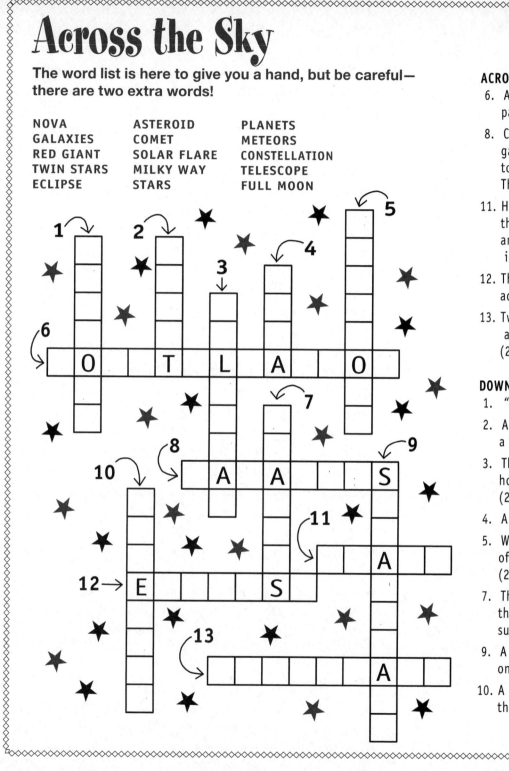

ACROSS

6. A picture seen in a pattern of stars

8. Collections of stars, gas, and dust held together by gravity. The Milky Way is one!

11. Huge balls of gas that produce light and heat. Our sun is one!

12. The Earth's shadow across the moon

13. Two stars in orbit around each other (2 words)

DOWN

1. "Shooting Stars"

2. A small, icy ball with a long, glowing tail

3. The galaxy that holds our solar system (2 words)

4. An exploding star

5. When the whole face of the moon is lit up (2 words)

7. The large spheres that orbit around our sun. Some have rings!

9. A powerful explosion on the sun (2 words)

10. A small rocky object that orbits the sun

The First Star I See Tonight!

Does it seem like there are a lot of faint stars when you look up at the sky? One reason this is true is because bright stars don't last very long. Usually a white dwarf star is one that has used up all its fuel. If this star is "running out of gas," how could it possibly become a nova that lights up the sky like fireworks and then go dim again? This happens because a nova has a companion star that pours its gas around the white dwarf until the surface of the dwarf star is burning again. Once the fuel is gone, so is the light. This second life can happen only once or it might happen many times, so keep an eye on the sky to see if you spot one! Would you think that a nova could be the brightest star in the sky? Many of the brightest stars are found in the constellations of the zodiac. Castor and Pollux are the two bright stars found in the well-known constellation of the Gemini twins. Another bright star is Aldebaran, which seems to form the eye of Taurus the bull. See if you can find Regulus, the bright star located at the base of Leo the lion's tail. There are several bright stars in the super bright constellation called Pleiades that are also known as the seven sisters. They would all be good places to look for the brightest star near us, but we don't have to travel very far or consult a star map in your newspaper to find the winner. If you guessed the brightest star close to Earth is the sun, you're right. Most people forget that the sun is a star. From here, the sun is very bright, but if you wanted to look at the sun from another galaxy, you would need a very strong telescope to see it! See how many people you can fool when you ask them the question, "Do stars only come out at night?" If they say, "Yes," ask them, "What about the sun?"

Happy Birthday to You

How would you like to see a bunch of baby stars? Many astronomers say that one of the "stars" in the belt of the constellation Orion is a nebula filled with pro-

The EVERYTHING KIDS Astronomy Book

tostars, which is the last step before a star is born or becomes a true star! For a star to survive, the pressure from the burning fuel pushing outward must equal the gravity pulling inward. Have you ever flown in a hot air balloon? The heat of the fire forces the balloon up while gravity tries to pull the balloon back to the ground. Although a star like the sun is not very big during the middle of its life, it is much, much larger when it is forming and while it is dying. Do you think the star's pressure change is what causes this to happen? If you said yes, you're right!

Orion has two giant stars in its constellation, a blue giant called Rigel and a red giant called Betelguese (pronounced beetle juice). Neither will have a long life as far as stars go. Huge stars like Rigel burn hotter and faster than a small star, so this red giant's hydrogen is almost gone and it is starting to burn its core. The original size of a giant star will determine if it will burn to a cinder or explode into a supernova when it reaches the iron core. Scientists believe the explosions are caused when the iron puts out the fire that was keeping up the pressure inside the star's core. Eventually gravity crushes it, then all of the contents, some too small to be seen, come rushing out.

Mapping the Stars

Have you ever watched an airport beacon's light sweeping through the air? Their beacons use many different combinations of

Found out in Space

Look carefully at this letter grid through your telescope. How many of the deep space objects from the word list can you find? Answers can go side to side, or up and down.

ASTEROID   METEOR   PULSAR

BLACK HOLE   MOON   RED GIANT

COMET   NEBULA   STAR

GALAXY   PLANET

```
T W I P U L S A R N
K G L E T W I N E K
L A S T E R O I D E
L L I T T L E S G A
A A R P H O B W I L
W X O L N D L E A U
W Y H A A T A Y N B
U A R N E U C P T E
M E T E O R K B O N
O E T T H E H W O R
O L D S O C O M E T
N E B U H L L I K E
A S T A R D E I A M
```

Sun or Star?

Any star the same size of Earth's sun or smaller is considered to be a dwarf star. The sun is known as a yellow dwarf star.

JUST for FUN

Pie in the Sky

How about a sky you can eat? All you need is a paper plate covered in whipped cream. Add a drop or two of blue food coloring and stir it with a spoon. To make your stars in the sky you can add marshmallows, candy pieces, cookie crumbs, or star shaped pieces of flavored gelatin. Then eat.

colors and rotating speeds of light to indicate what type of airport it is. Astronomers found a new type of variable star in the constellation Cepheus that pulsates like these beacons, which helps to tell them what type of star it is. A Cepheid is a star that is unstable because it is slowly dying. Its temperature, size, and radiation are causing its brightness to change at a regular rate, but the rate or period of brightness is not the same for every star. Once astronomers learn a star is in a Cepheid stage and how long its pulsation period is, they can calculate how far away it is. This is just one more way of measuring the immense distances to the stars. Other methods are:

1. Using radar within the solar system.
2. Calculating increasing distances using geometry.
3. Comparing the brightness of different stars.
4. Figuring out the speed of rotating galaxies.
5. Photographing the explosions of the supernovae.

Because of all of this, in less than a century astronomers have progressed from believing that the sun was the center of the universe to learning that the universe extends for somewhere close to 13 billion light years. If you remember each light year is about 6 trillion miles, how many total miles is that? Will your calculator handle that many numbers?

Chapter 9

Is There Anybody Out There?

All of the elements on Earth, some of which must be manufactured in a laboratory, can be found in the radiation from stars measured by the spectroscopes or cameras mounted on telescopes. They are all formed when stars die.

Many people would like to believe that there is life on some of the other planets or somewhere else in the universe. Movies, TV shows, and lots of books have been produced to show how different life on Earth might be after a visit from a few aliens in UFOs. People on Earth listen for signals, send messages on space probes, and try to develop quicker ways to travel in space. If there is intelligent life out there, they hope that some day, some way, they can go visit them.

Phone Calls to Outer Space

Have you ever wondered what it would be like to talk to somebody or something that is from out of this world? The people at SETI (Search for Extra-Terrestrial Intelligence) have a lot of people who are willing to help them look for aliens. Astronomers with huge radio telescopes receive signals from the stars in space all the time, but the scientists at SETI are searching for signals that change, similar to a code you might use to talk to a friend. Over the years, many people have volunteered to help search for these unusual signals. The SETI project connected these people's home computers through the Internet to check out and sort the information the telescopes obtain. Do you think these astronomers are searching the skies to communicate with other people in the solar system, since extraterrestrial means not of this Earth? Or do you think they are hoping to visit with an alien from outer space? Even if SETI eventually receives any signals, the one trying to communicate will probably no longer exist.

Collect Call

An astronomer at SETI has just received the very first message from outer space! He tried to email the news to his friends, but in his excitement, the astronomer put his hands on the keyboard in the wrong position. Now the message looks like a bunch of jibberish! Use the keyboard below to decode the message.

Y8? Y92 Q43 697P

DQH 23 G94492 Q D7*

9R W7TQ4 *O3QW3P

Are you <u>sure</u> this is the right message?

I checked it <u>twice</u>!

FUN FACT

Upside-Down Stars

Most telescopes see stars upside down, unlike binoculars. Telescopes come in all shapes and sizes. Some are so big that the astronomers have to travel up the telescope to reach the eyepiece at the top.

It takes a long time for light and radio waves to travel any distance in space. SETI is hoping another friendly being from the distant galaxy will still be waiting for a return phone call from Earth!

Speed of Sound

Do you like thunderstorms? Most of the time a flash of lightning is followed by a loud clap of thunder unless the storm is too far away. Sometimes all you see is the light flickering in the distance, which is also known as heat lightning. If you count 1,001, 1,002, etc. between the flash and the boom, you can estimate how far away the storm is. So why does it take longer to hear the thunder? Sound travels through the atmosphere at about 1,000 feet per second while light travels at 186,000 miles per second. It is pretty easy to guess which one will get there first. Strange as it may seem, the temperature of the air and how high up in the atmosphere the sound is will also affect how fast it travels.

Can Sound Get Wet?

Do you think sound travels faster or slower in water? If you want to find out, have one of your parents stand at one end of your local swimming pool while you make a noise in the air above and below the water at the other end. Which one of the sounds traveled faster? If you lived in space, you wouldn't be able to hear any noise at all because sound waves can't travel where there is no atmosphere. As a rocket leaves the atmosphere, do you think it would sound more like someone turning the volume down on a radio or do you think the sound would just slowly fade away? The lack of sound in space was a big problem for the astronauts who were trying to communicate when they went out there. To solve the problem scientists installed radios in the spacesuits of the astronauts so they could talk to each other and to their mission control center hear on Earth.

Unidentified Flying Objects

Do you believe in UFOs? Have you ever seen a really bright object in the sky and gotten really excited about it until a grownup told you it was Venus or even the space station orbiting Earth? If you would like to know when and where the space station and the Hubble Space Telescope will be passing over your part of the world, type in "Spaceflight1" in the search box on your Internet. Over a hundred years ago, authors like H.G. Wells started writing books about visitors from other worlds. Almost sixty years ago, pilots thought they were seeing flying saucers and a lot of people still believe they visit Earth from time to time. Many people think what they are actually seeing are weather balloons, funny shaped clouds, or new types of aircraft.

What do you think a real UFO would look like? Why wouldn't they be shaped more like the rockets that astronauts pilot today? Have you ever thought about how many times science fiction writers almost seem to predict the future when they wrote about things like flying machines, submarines, and spaceships landing on the moon? Now that we have flying machines and submarines, it makes you wonder if spaceships may visit Earth someday. Some people like to think these aliens might look like some of the strange creatures living here on Earth while others think they would look more like a person. Who knows, but life on other planets could look more like our dinosaurs or other mammals. Just think what past travelers would have seen if they landed here on Earth millions of years ago. Although we think of ourselves as astronauts or explorers when we travel out into space, would we be considered aliens if we landed on another planet or moon?

JUST for FUN

Can You Hear Me?

Try taping your voice on a recorder and then playing it back. Do you sound the same as the recording? Why not ask a friend to see if they know it is your voice. Then record several people and see if they can guess who is who. Now try listening with a pair of earmuffs covering your ears.

Try This

Edible Aliens

Using the recipe on the flavored gelatin box, make a batch of jiggly green aliens. Once the gelatin is solid, cut out your aliens using a gingerbread man cookie cutter. Then add on your alien's eyes, hair, etc. using whipped cream and candy or squeeze cheese and shredded vegetables. Don't forget to invite someone to join in the fun!

Silly Science Fiction

Ask a friend or family member to help create this silly science fiction story. Don't show them the story first! Just ask them for the kind of word you need for each blank spot (a description is written underneath). Write the words your helper gives you in the blanks, then read the story out loud. HINT: Use a pencil so you can erase the words and play again!

_____ was driving home. It was dark. There were
     a friend's name

_____ stars in the sky, and the moon was _____
big number   *shape*

and bright. Suddenly, a _____ and _____ beam
                               color   *another color*

of light appeared. Standing in the light was a _____,
                                                          adjective

and _____ creature! It looked at _____
         adjective   *same friend's name*

and said "My name is _____. I have come from
                           nonsense word

Planet _____ in the _____ Nebula.
      another nonsense word   *funny animal*

I have been traveling for _____ years. I could really
                                 large number

use a bag of _____ and a _____!"
             snack food   *kind of drink*

Unsolved Alien Mysteries Here on Earth

There are some people who believe that when a UFO takes off from a cornfield, it leaves behind a perfect circle of chopped corn stalks called a crop circle. It's fun to think that you can prove that aliens are visiting Earth, but why are they never seen arriving or leaving the spot? Some people believe that aliens have visited Earth many times in the past. Their proof, they believe, is the pyramids in Egypt and the Americas, the enormous drawings of animals in Peru, the huge figures on Easter Island, and the legendary continent of Atlantis. They try to convince other people that they were all created with the aid of extraterrestrials or aliens because no one else could have had the strength and intelligence to create these wonders.

If the people living so long ago were smart enough to predict eclipses and the movements of the planets and stars just from the records they kept, couldn't they have thought of a way to move the huge blocks of stone that made the pyramids? It may have been possible since the famous astronomer Archimedes was using pulleys and levers to raise heavy loads thousands of years ago. Have you ever watched someone loading a truck? They usually lay boards with one end on the ground and the other end lying in the truck, then they roll their loads upward, instead of lifting them. How long do you suppose people have been doing this? For years we have looked to the skies and space to answer all sorts of unknown things. Maybe aliens were invented to explain all of these mysteries like the mythical gods were so many years ago.

Cool Jobs

Have you ever worked on a science project with your classmates? It is amazing what you can accomplish

Try This

Unidentified Flying Objects

You can make your own UFOs by placing two foil pie pans with their rims together, then taping them. You can also try using paper bowls or plates. Which object flies the best? Can you think of any other things that might fly better? How about making a rocket on a string by running a cord through a paper towel tube?

when you are part of a team. Look what the astronomers throughout history have found out as they kept building on other scientists' work. You don't have be an actual astronomer to help in the study of outer space. If you want to work in the field of astronomy there are many interesting jobs to consider, including the ones these people do:

- Mathematicians who figure out what kind of stars the astronomers have found.
- Lecturers who talk at observatories and planetariums.
- Engineers who build and maintain all the types of telescopes.
- Technicians who collect, develop, and sort all the pictures taken by the telescopes.
- Computer programmers, geologists, chemists, and probably the job that most people think would be the most fun, astronaut.

It may surprise you to learn that many astronauts have the training to do many of these jobs, before they enter the space program. For fun, the National Aeronautics and Space Administration (NASA) opened a space camp for kids so they could try out some of the exciting things real astronauts do, like floating around in a room without any gravity. Many astronauts started dreaming about going into space when they were young. With a lot of work and training, dreams can come true!

If They Won't Come to Us, We'll Go to Them!

If you wanted a friend to come to visit you and they lived far, far away, you would probably send them a map so they wouldn't get lost. If they lived in another country and knew very little about where you lived, you might send them information about what to expect when they got here. If they didn't speak your language, you might have to draw pictures. When people travel in different countries they use road signs that have pictures as well as writing. When scientists on Earth started sending out space probes, they sent along discs that had maps of the sky containing certain stars that showed where Earth was located. They sent along songs and information about life here on Earth. All of the information was recorded in many languages. Astronomers using the Hubble telescope have found new planets in other galaxies and they are hoping they will find more. The information sent on these probes called Voyager 1 and 2 may never reach intelligent life forms in outer space, but think how exciting it would be if these terrestrial messages reached someone in space and they answered back. If you were going to send a message to outer space, what would you say? Would you write it in just one language or several different languages and how would you send it? Would you send pictures, drawings, or recorded words or music?

Home Away from Home

Would you like to have a job that takes you hundreds of thousands of miles from home? One day in the future people may be living and working on the moon. Some scientists are talking about setting up a colony there; it would be like living in a very large space station! Maybe they will use it as a launch site for trips to Mars or a base for telescopes away from the light and radio waves coming from Earth. Or maybe they will use it as a tourist attraction. The astronauts say the Earthrises (sort of like our sunrises) are

JUST for FUN

Let's Go to the Movies

One way to take a trip into outer space without ever leaving your house is to watch a science fiction movie about aliens or traveling through the universe. All you need is a few friends or family members, some popcorn, something to drink, a comfy chair, and a good movie. How many famous movies about space can you name?

Try This

Pretty Flashy

How about borrowing someone's strobe light? The beam of light or beacon that they produce moves very fast, like some of the items in space. You can change the setting on the strobe light to move slowly like an airport or lighthouse beacon or quickly like a pulsar. Can you move around the room when the light is flashing?

beautiful. If you don't like the long days of winter, a job on the far side of moon sure wouldn't be for you. Getting so many rays on the near side probably wouldn't be that much fun, either. Just imagine living in a place where the outside temperature varies at least 400 degrees F. It gets close to 300 degrees F. below zero. And you thought Antarctica was cold! Someone would have to keep reminding everyone to be sure and keep their spacesuits zipped up if they went outside. They probably would also have to remind them that there would be no running or jumping because of the thin atmosphere. If you're wondering if they would have to dodge a lot of meteorites, the scientists say there seems to be a lot fewer of them than there used to be.

An Endless Mission

Would you like to be the first astronaut to walk on Mars? It wouldn't be the same as just hopping on the school bus. Even after you completed your astronaut's training, you might have to wait until they built a launch site on the moon. It's much easier to jump on the moon and it is also easier to lift off for a spaceship. Can you guess why? If you thought it was due to the weak gravity, you're right! Maybe you have watched the Mars rovers traveling over its surface. How do you think NASA managed to send them hundreds of thousands of miles and then six months later have them land exactly where they wanted them? It's a lot like football players who throw the ball to where they think the other running player will be; they figure out when the rovers' spaceship will meet with Mars as its orbit nears Earth. They could probably send men to Mars, but what would they do about the supplies they would need for the long wait until they were once again near Earth's orbit? Astronauts in the space shuttle and the space station have learned to live in small spaces; they enjoy floating in the zero gravity, sleeping upside down, and throwing orange juice bubbles. How would you like to live with your friends every day for at least two years? It will probably be many more years before you have to be worrying about traveling to another galaxy, but who would have guessed that we would ever travel to the moon?

Journey into Space

Imagine what it must be like to take off into space. Astronauts who have traveled into space always talk about the view. From five miles up, you can see Interstate highways, large buildings, and rivers. But what do you think you would be able to see on Earth if you were actually on your way to the moon? Astronauts report seeing continents, really large rivers, and even the Great Wall of China! One of the best parts of being an astronaut is seeing the world from a different point of view, which few people ever get to see. Although there is a great deal of work to do on a mission, the astronauts are allowed a certain amount of time to sit and gaze at our planet. As they return from their mission and get closer to Earth, they begin to see more details like mountains and rivers, and eventually they get close enough to see houses and people. Even though you aren't traveling to space, you can take a closer look at this one-of-a-kind planet. Have you ever really looked at ants in an anthill, busily working away in their small world? Or how about watching what goes on in a nearby patch of flowers. You can learn more about Earth by using microscopes and binoculars to see what you might not have noticed at first glance. What does a piece of bread, a coin, or your skin look like under a magnifying glass?

Another World?

Recently scientists have discovered that a planet in a different solar system far away from ours may contain water in its atmosphere. This new information gives them hope that they will find other planets capable of supporting life someday.

Sailing Off in Space

The Russians call their space travelers cosmonauts, which means "sailors in the universe." In the United States, they prefer to call their travelers astronauts, which means "sailors to the stars."

TIME WARP: Some scientists wonder if there are places in space where time is distorted or warped. One place they believe a time warp may exist is in or around a black hole. Because no one has ever been there they can only guess what might happen.

Traveling Through Time

Do you ever wish that you were old enough to drive a car or go to college? If you could, would you just travel forward to those exciting times in a time machine like the people did in the book written by Jules Verne? In a way you actually do when you look up into the night sky. Many of the stars that you and the astronomers are looking at are no longer there; they were created and then ceased to exist billions of years ago. The diminishing light or explosion from their death just hasn't reached Earth! Astronomers believe that light from a star may just disappear, sucked in by all the gravity created by those massive black holes. A scientist named Albert Einstein believes that a time warp can happen as anything nears these holes, and that time and space are stretched like your body is when you look in the mirror in a fun house at an amusement park! If you were traveling in a spaceship and you passed around the edge of these whirlpools in space, would time slow down or speed up? No one knows for sure, because it's only a theory, but wouldn't it be fun if it were true? Eventually, we may solve all of the mysteries outer space has to offer, but until then it is fun to wonder about them.

Space of Tomorrow?

In the beginning, people only dreamed of living in space. Before they could live there, first they would have to find a way to get off the ground. Not only did we get off the ground, but today many people take turns living and working in space stations for up to a year or so at a time. How would you like to live in a traveling space hotel, like some people believe may happen someday? Will it ever be possible for mankind to live forever in a rocket type of mobile home, touring space and discovering the answers to all of our questions about time and space? Our adventures in space

Hello UFOs!

The Hubble Space Telescope took pictures of these UFOs on two different nights. Which two spacecraft do not appear in both pictures?

may be just beginning. Who knows what secrets we might learn from time warps, stardust, or how a lack of gravity will affect us? Does outer space hold the key to the fountain of youth, or will we find some of the cures for our diseases? Will we find new foods or materials to make new things out of? We can only imagine what we will learn as we spend more time living away from our world and traveling closer to other ones. No one really knows for sure what lies ahead, which is why they call it space exploration. Years ago, people may have thought they knew all there was to know about space, yet new discoveries are still being made, and people go on dreaming of what the future may hold. Maybe one day you will find out for yourself what lies beyond the nearest star.

Glossary

alien
Beings thought to live somewhere else out in space are called aliens. No one is sure if there is any other life in the universe, other than here on Earth. Another name for an alien is an extraterrestrial.

asteroid
An asteroid is a small object similar in several ways to a planet. Many asteroids are made of rock and orbit the sun.

astrology
A belief that stars and other objects in space can be used to predict future happenings or events. People who are born under certain signs are expected to have certain characteristics and qualities.

astronaut
Explorers who travel out into space are known as astronauts. Some astronauts have become famous for taking the first steps in space or being the first woman or man to leave the Earth's atmosphere.

astronomy
The study of all things in space. The people who watch the skies for new stars or planets or changes in the ones that have already been discovered are called astronomers. Astronomy is a type of science.

atmosphere
The gases contained around an object in space are called its *atmosphere.* Earth's atmosphere contains a combination of gases that produce the air we breathe.

aurora
One of nature's most spectacular light shows is called an aurora. These light shows take place close to the Northern and Southern Poles as solar particles collide with the earth's magnetic fields.

axis
Like a top, each planet has a center line known as an axis that it revolves around. Earth's axis would run from its North Pole straight through to its South Pole.

comet
A comet is an object that appears to have a glowing tail as it travels through space. One famous comet is Halley's comet, known for its timely return trips.

constellation
A group of stars that together form an image in the sky. One constellation that is well known is Orion.

dwarf planet
A planet that is smaller in size than the other planets it is being compared to. Pluto is considered a dwarf planet because it is so much smaller than the other planets in our solar system.

eclipse
When an object in space blocks the light of another object or prevents it from being in view, it is called an eclipse. Two common eclipses are solar and lunar.

galaxy

A large group of stars out in space. There are numerous galaxies in the universe. Galaxies can come in different shapes and sizes. The galaxy we live in is a spiral galaxy.

gravity

The force that pulls things toward the earth. There is also a gravitational force in many other areas throughout the universe that seems to hold things together.

lunar

A word that describes something that has to do with the moon. There are lunar calendars and lunar missions. If people lived on the moon it would be a lunar colony.

magnitude

The amount of light a star emits or gives off is called its magnitude. Astronomers measure the magnitude of the stars out in the universe by using a number system.

meteorite

The objects that fall from space onto the earth are called meteorites. When they start to burn in the sky, they are sometimes called falling stars.

meteorology

The study of the Earth's atmosphere, usually involving activities within it such as the weather. Someone who studies meteorology is called a meteorologist.

Milky Way

The spiral galaxy that appears in our sky, like a faint trail of spilled milk, is called the Milky Way. The Milky Way is made up of billions of stars.

myth

A traditional story that is usually based on beliefs from religion or history. Myths have been told for years along with similar stories like tall tales, fables, and fairy tales.

nebula

Nebulae can be both light and dark, depending on whether a star is shining on the nebula's dust or whether the nebula's dust is blocking the light from the star that is behind it.

Oort cloud

A type of cloud that encircles our solar system. This cloud is believed to be the birthplace of some of the icy comets that can be found traveling through our solar system.

phase

When something changes or develops, it goes through phases or stages. Each month the moon goes through a cycle of phases from a new moon to a full moon and back again. A crescent moon is one of the phases in the moon's cycle.

planetarium

A special building designed to display all the wonders of the solar system and outer space to an audience.

Polaris

The name given to the earth's pole star. You can find Polaris by looking for a bright star in the northern sky. It is part of a constellation we call the Little Dipper.

reflecting

Normally, people are thinking of water or mirrors when they think about something reflecting an image or light. Even though the moon has no light source of its own, it shines in the sky because the sun's light is reflecting off of the moon's surface.

satellite

A satellite can be a manmade object or something created in space that orbits planets such as Earth. Manmade satellites are used to send information from place to place or keep track of the weather.

science fiction

When a story is made up or not true it is considered fiction. Science fiction is a blend of scientific information and fiction. Many stories and movies about space are considered science fiction.

solar system

Our solar system consists of eight planets, one dwarf planet, the sun, and all of the other items that orbit around it. Our solar system is just one of many in the universe.

spectrum

Scientists and astronomers use a spectroscope to see the breakdown or separation of light into a spectrum, the same colors created by light shining through a prism.

telescope

A telescope is a tool that was invented to help people see things that are far away in the distance. Astronomers use telescopes to see planets and stars millions of miles out in space.

time warp

Some scientists wonder if there are places in space where time is distorted or warped. One place they believe a time warp may exist is in or around a black hole. Because no one has ever been there they can only guess what might happen.

universe

Everything around us as far as the eye can see. It contains stars, galaxies, planets, space, and us. Some people think there are other universes that go on beyond the one where we live.

Resources

Books

Carson, Mary Kay. *Exploring the Solar System: A History with 22 Activities* (For Kids series). Chicago Review Press, 2006.

Cole, Michael D. *The Sun: The Center of the Solar System* (Countdown to Space). Enslow Publishers, 2001.

DK Publishing (editor). *Astronomy.* DK Publishing, 2004.

DK Publishing (editor). *Universe* (DK Eyewitness Books). DK Publishing, 2003.

Harrington, Philip. *Astronomy for All Ages, 2nd edition: Discovering the Universe through Activities for Children and Adults.* Globe Pequot, 2000.

Kerrod, Robin. *Astronomy.* Southwater Publishing, 2000.

Nobleman, Marc Tyler. *3-D Thrillers! Solar System* (Discovery Kids). Dutton Children's Books, 2001.

School Specialty Publishing (editor). *Our Solar System Science Kit* (Brighter Child). School Specialty Publishing, 2004.

School Specialty Publishing (editor). *Solar System* (Just the Facts). School Specialty Publishing, 2006.

Sohn, Emily. *Space and Astronomy* (Science News for Kids). Chelsea House Publications, 2006.

Stott, Carole. *Astronomy: Discoveries, Solar System, Stars, Universe.* Kingfisher, 2003.

VanCleave, Janice. *Janice VanCleave's the Solar System: Mind-Boggling Experiments You Can Turn into Science Fair Projects.* Jossey-Bass, 2000.

Web Sites

Amazing Space
At Amazing Space you will find movies featuring current cosmic events, along with space games, news about the universe, and a section for homework help.
http://amazing-space.stsci.edu/tonights_sky/ index.php

Artyastro.com
At Artyastro.com you can travel through space, enter a time machine, or check your weight on one of the many different planets. You will also find word search pages when you visit this site.
www.artyastro.com/main.htm

Astronomy for Kids
This site is filled with all kinds of fun things like sky maps, wonders from outer space, electronic postcards, information on the constellations, and endless space facts.
www.dustbunny.com/afk

Earth and Moon Viewer
One way to see the earth and the moon up close is to use this site called the Earth and Moon Viewer. You can simply click on one of several preset images or you can see the

latitude and longitude for anywhere you want to explore on Earth. See the world from the sun's point of view at the link below.

http://fourmilab.ch/earthview/vplanet.html

Earth from Space
You can visit Earth from space by clicking on this large map to see the world the way a satellite sees it.

http://earth.jsc.nasa.gov/sseop/efs/categories.htm

Exploratorium
This Web site allows you to calculate your weight or age in numerous places located in space. You can also test your knowledge of gravity.

www.exploratorium.edu/ronh/weight/index.html

KidsAstronomy.com
You will find all kinds of things to do at KidsAstronomy.com. Here you can print your own copy of a star map, play a constellation finding game, mail free e-cards, listen to songs, and see beautiful images.

www.kidsastronomy.com

NASA Kids' Club
NASA Kids' Club offers hours of entertaining fun on many different levels. Challenge yourself and your family's knowledge of the universe with these astronomical activities.

www.nasa.gov/audience/forkids/kidsclub/flash/index.html

NASA Science Fun
With one click of your mouse and a tap of your space bar you can watch numerous movies of all different kinds of space phenomena.

http://science.hq.nasa.gov/kids

NASA Space Place
NASA Space Place contains numerous projects, facts, games, and endless animated information. You will also find crafts, poetry, and recipes at the link below.

http://spaceplace.nasa.gov/en/kids

National Geographic
National Geographic lets you explore our solar system in 3-D. Each view also contains lots of fun facts and information about the planets.

www.nationalgeographic.com/solarsystem/splash.html

Science News for Kids
Explore new worlds when you visit Science News for Kids. Here you will find the latest astronomy updates, fun games, and lots of brainteasers.

www.sciencenewsforkids.org/pages/search.asp?catid=31

Space World
At Space World you will find quizzes, a dictionary, maps, numerous links to other sites, and information on everything from the phases of the moon to how to make a model of the solar system.

www.gigglepotz.com/space.htm

Windows to the Universe
See if you can eliminate all the junk left out in space in one of the numerous games available on this Windows to the Universe site. There are several puzzles, games, stories, myths, and even a virtual coloring book all just a click away.

www.windows.ucar.edu

World Almanac for Kids

When you visit World Almanac for Kids you will find several interactive diagrams of our solar system along with a variety of games, quizzes, information, history, and an electronic dictionary.

www.worldalmanacforkids.com/explore/space.html

Yahoo! Kids

This site has incredible videos, fun jokes, awesome pictures, and a place to find the answers to many of your questions about space.

http://kids.yahoo.com/science

Appendix C
Puzzle Answers

Chapter 1

Going Backwards? • *page 3*

How Big Is Big? • *page 4*

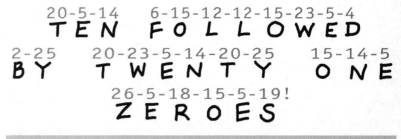

20-5-14   6-15-12-12-15-23-5-4
TEN FOLLOWED
2-25   20-23-5-14-20-25   15-14-5
BY   TWENTY   ONE
26-5-18-15-5-19!
ZEROES

10,000,000,000,000,000,000,000

One in a Billion • *page 9*

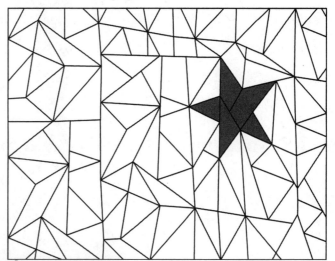

Sweet Scientists • *page 11*

What are astronomers' favorite candies?

Milky Way Bar

Mars Bar

Starlight Mint

Chapter 2

Around and Around We Go • *page 18*

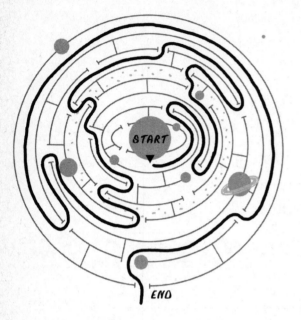

Ribbons of Light • *page 22*

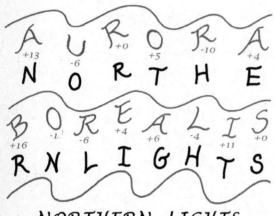

NORTHERN LIGHTS

Free Vacation • *page 25*

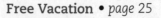
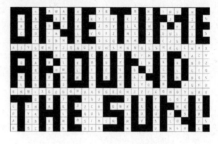

Chapter 3

Go to Jail • *page 30*

He proved that the earth was not the center of the solar system.

Patience Please! • *page 36*

ASTRONOMERS DON'T MAKE THINGS HAPPEN — THEY WAIT AND WATCH WHAT HAPPENS

The EVERYTHING KIDS' Astronomy Book

You Are Here • *page 39*

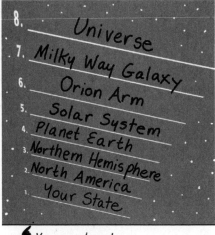

8. Universe
7. Milky Way Galaxy
6. Orion Arm
5. Solar System
4. Planet Earth
3. Northern Hemisphere
2. North America
1. Your State

You are here!

Chapter 4

Always Changing • *page 44*

○ **F U L L** *moon*
39 = full of light

◐ **G I B B O U S** *moon*
60 = between full and half

◑ **H A L F** *moon*
22 = half light, half dark

◕ **C R E S C E N T** *moon*
67 = a sliver of light

● **N E W** *moon*
32 = all dark

Crazy Moon • *page 49*

How Many Moons? • *page 52*

   8   number of planets in our solar system

+ **1**   number of dwarf planets named "Pluto"

+ **24** number of hours for one Earth rotation

+ **12** number of full moons in a year

x **2**   number of years in 24 months

- **10** number of letters in "moon phases"

= **80** number of moons to make one Earth

Chapter 5

Go Mercury! • *page 59*

=*Mercury circles the*
=*sun faster than any*
=*other planet in the*
=*solar system – only*
=*eighty-eight days!*

Mystery on Mars • *page 61*

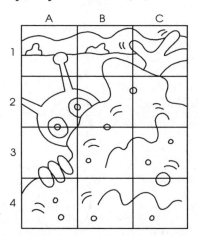

Appendix C: Puzzle Answers

Deathly Dry • *page 65*

THERE IS MORE WATER
IN THE SAHARA DESERT
THAN ON ALL OF VENUS

Chapter 6

The Big Bucket • *page 70*

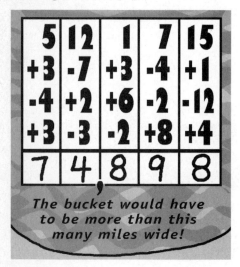

5	12	1	7	15
+3	-7	+3	-4	+1
-4	+2	+6	-2	-12
+3	-3	-2	+8	+4
7	4	8	9	8

7 4, 8 9 8

The bucket would have to be more than this many miles wide!

Long Journey • *page 73*

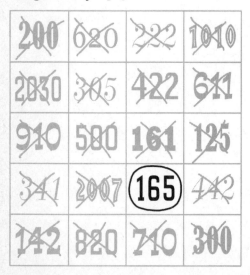

Poor Pluto! • *page 77*

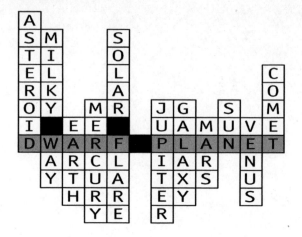

How many astronomers does it take to change a lightbulb? • *page 78*

None. Astronomers can see stars better when it is dark!

The EVERYTHING KIDS· Astronomy Book

Chapter 7

Name That Nebula • *page 85*

1. Horsehead
2. Boomerang
3. Fish on a Platter
4. Duck
5. Thumbprint
6. Apple Core
7. Running Chicken
8. Cat's Eye
9. Ghosthead

Oops! • *page 89*

First you must turn the book a quarter turn counterclockwise. Then hold the book so that the bottom edge of the puzzle is close to your eye, and the top edge is titled away from your eye. Squint one eye closed, and look down the length of the puzzle. Tilt the book up and down a little until all of a sudden you get the perfect angle, and you can read the answer!

Confusing Comets • *page 91*

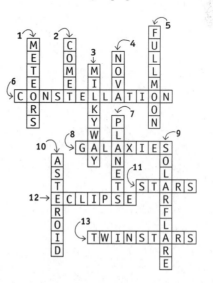

Chapter 8

Picture in the Sky • *page 97*

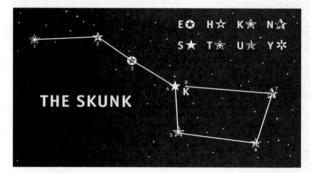

THE SKUNK

Twin Stars • *page 99*

Across the Sky • *page 101*

1. METEORS
2. COMET
3. MILKYWAY
4. NOVA
5. FULLMOON
6. CONSTELLATION
7. PLANET
8. GALAXIES
9. SOLARFLARE
10. ASTEROID
11. STARS
12. ECLIPSE
13. TWINSTARS

Found out in Space • *page 103*

```
T W I P U L S A R N
K G L E T W I N E K
L A S T E R O I D E
L L I T T L E S G A
A A R P H O B W I L
W X O L N D L E A U
W Y H A A T A Y N B
U A R N E U C P T E
M E T E O R K B O N
O E T T H E H W O R
O L D S O C O M E T
N E B U H L L I K E
A S T A R D E I A M
```

Silly Science Fiction • *page 110*

Everyone will have a different story. Here's ours!

<u>KELLY</u> was driving home. It was dark. There were
a friend's name

<u>125,314</u> stars in the sky, and the moon was <u>SQUARE</u>
big number *shape*

and bright. Suddenly, a <u>PINK</u> and <u>ORANGE</u> beam
color *another color*

of light appeared. Standing in the light was a <u>SLIMY</u>,
adjective

and <u>WRINKLED</u> creature! It looked at <u>KELLY</u>
adjective *same friend's name*

and said "My name is <u>BLORK</u>. I have come from
nonsense word

Planet <u>ZUPNARK</u> in the <u>PLATYPUS</u> Nebula.
another nonsense word *funny animal*

I have been traveling for <u>20 MILLION</u> years. I could really
large number

use a bag of <u>CHEESE POPS</u> and a <u>ROOT BEER</u> !"
snack food *kind of drink*

Chapter 9

Collect Call • *page 107*

Hi! How are you?
Y8? Y92 Q43 697P

Can we borrow a cup
DQH 23 G94492 Q D7*

of sugar please?
9R W7TQ4 *03QW3P

Hello UFOs! • *page 117*

The **EVERYTHING KIDS'** Astronomy Book

Index

A
Air, 19–21
Aldrin, Edwin "Buzz," 52, 53
Aliens, 108, 109, 111, 119
Andromeda Galaxy, 6
Archimedes, 111
Armstrong, Neil, 52
Asteroids, 87–88, 119
Astrology, 97, 102, 119
Astronauts, 43, 50–53, 112, 119
Astronomers, 4, 6, 12, 30, 36, 111–12
Astronomy, 4, 119
Atmosphere, 19–21, 37, 119
Atmospheric pressure, 20–21
Aurora, 33, 119
Aurora australis, 33
Aurora borealis, 22, 33
Axis, 71, 119

B
"Big Bang," 3, 10, 12
Big Dipper, 28
Black holes, 84, 86

C
Carbon dioxide, 34, 37, 58, 62
Centrifugal force, 8
Colors, 10, 17, 19, 26, 65–66, 72
Comets, 89, 90–92, 119
Constellations, 28, 95–98, 100, 102–4, 119
Copernicus, 6
Craters, 40, 42, 43, 45

D
Daytime, 26, 37
Doppler effect, 38
Dwarf planet, 68, 75, 119
Dwarf star, 102, 104

E
Earth, 27–40
Earth, formation of, 31–32
Earth, layers of, 32–33
Earth, needs of, 16, 34–35
Earth, orbit of, 34, 37
Earth, rotation of, 8, 21, 26, 46
Earthquakes, 32
Eclipses, 24, 26, 37, 119
Einstein, Albert, 16, 116
Electricity, 29–31
Electromagnetic waves, 29–31
Equator, 23
Extra-Terrestrial Intelligence, 106–8

F
Fusion, 15

G
Gagarin, Yuri, 51
Galaxies, 5–6, 10–11, 39, 119–20
Galileo, 6, 30, 76
Glaciers, 37, 40
Glenn, John, 51–52
Glossary, 119–21
Glow-in-the-dark galaxy, 5
Grand Canyon, 40
Gravity, of Earth, 8–9, 12, 14, 120
Gravity, of moon, 43, 46

H
Halley's comet, 91–92
Halo, 19, 43, 86
Hipparchus, 94
Hubble telescope, 64, 78, 109, 113
Hydrogen, 37

The Everything® KIDS' Series!

Packed with tons of information, activities, and puzzles, the Everything® Kids' books are perennial bestsellers that keep kids active and engaged.

Each book is $7.95, two-color, 8" x 9¼", and 144 –176 pages.

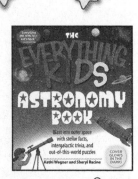

The Everything® Kids'
Astronomy Book
ISBN 10: 1-59869-544-4

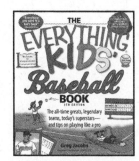

The Everything® Kids' Baseball
Book, 5th Ed.
ISBN 10: 1-59869-487-1

The Everything® Kids' Connect the Dots
Puzzle and Activity Book
ISBN 10: 1-59869-647-5

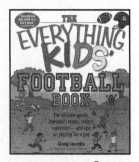

The Everything® Kids'
Football Book
ISBN 10: 1-59869-565-7

The Everything® Kids' Learning
French Book
ISBN 10: 1-59869-543-6

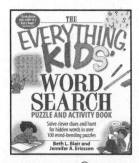

The Everything® Kids' Word
Search Puzzle and Activity Book
ISBN 10: 1-59869-545-2

A silly, goofy, and undeniably icky addition to the Everything® Kids' series . . .

The Everything® Kids'

GROSS
Series

Chock-full of sickening entertainment for hours of disgusting fun.

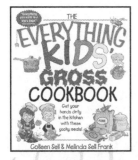
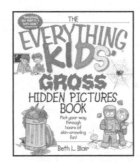

Other Everything® Kids' Titles Available

The Everything® Kids' Animal Puzzle & Activity Book
1-59337-305-8

The Everything® Kids' Baseball Book, 4th Ed.
1-59337-614-6

The Everything® Kids' Bible Trivia Book
1-59337-031-8

The Everything® Kids' Bugs Book
1-58062-892-3

The Everything® Kids' Cars and Trucks
Puzzle and Activity Book
1-59337-703-7

The Everything® Kids' Christmas Puzzle
& Activity Book
1-58062-965-2

The Everything® Kids' Cookbook
1-58062-658-0

The Everything® Kids' Crazy Puzzles Book
1-59337-361-9

The Everything® Kids' Dinosaurs Book
1-59337-360-0

The Everything® Kids' Environment Book
1-59869-670-X

The Everything® Kids' Fairies Puzzle and Activity Book
1-59869-394-8

The Everything® Kids' First Spanish Puzzle and
Activity Book
1-59337-717-7

The Everything® Kids' Halloween Puzzle &
Activity Book
1-58062-959-8

The Everything® Kids' Hidden Pictures Book
1-59337-128-4

The Everything® Kids' Horses Book
1-59337-608-1

The Everything® Kids' Joke Book
1-58062-686-6

The Everything® Kids' Knock Knock Book
1-59337-127-6

The Everything® Kids' Learning Spanish Book
1-59337-716-9

The Everything® Kids' Magical Science Experiments Book
1-59869-426-X

The Everything® Kids' Math Puzzles Book
1-58062-773-0

The Everything® Kids' Mazes Book
1-58062-558-4

The Everything® Kids' Money Book
1-58062-685-8

The Everything® Kids' Nature Book
1-58062-684-X

The Everything® Kids' Pirates Puzzle and Activity Book
1-59337-607-3

The Everything® Kids' Presidents Book
1-59869-262-3

The Everything® Kids' Princess Puzzle and Activity Book
1-59337-704-5

The Everything® Kids' Puzzle Book
1-58062-687-4

The Everything® Kids' Racecars Puzzle and Activity Book
1-59869-243-7

The Everything® Kids' Riddles & Brain Teasers Book
1-59337-036-9

The Everything® Kids' Science Experiments Book
1-58062-557-6

The Everything® Kids' Sharks Book
1-59337-304-X

The Everything® Kids' Soccer Book
1-58062-642-4

The Everything® Kids' Spies Puzzle and Activity Book
1-59869-409-X

The Everything® Kids' States Book
1-59869-263-1

The Everything® Kids' Travel Activity Book
1-58062-641-6

All titles are $6.95 or $7.95 unless otherwise noted.

Available wherever books are sold!
To order, call 800-258-0929, or visit us at *www.adamsmedia.com*
Everything® and everything.com® are registered trademarks of F+W Publications, Inc.
Prices subject to change without notice.